Tea for Two...
...with no cups

Polly Benge

Edited by Dan Hiscocks
Published by TravellersEye

Tea for Two ... with no cups
1st Edition
Published by TravellersEye Ltd
May 2000

Head Office:
60B High Street
Bridgnorth
Shropshire
WV16 4DX
United Kingdom
tel: (0044) 1746 766447
fax: (0044) 1746 766665
email: books@travellerseye.com
website: www.travellerseye.com

Set in Times
ISBN: 0953057593
Copyright 2000 Polly Benge

Printed and bound in Great Britain by Creative Print & Design Group.

For Mum and Dad

ACKNOWLEDGMENTS

I would like to say thanks to Lee Shale and Tracey Horseman without whom the trip would not have been possible. To my sister Sophie for her support, Peel Hunt for the use of their office equipment and Dan Hiscocks and Jill Ibberson at TravellersEye for their time, patience and faith.

CONTENTS

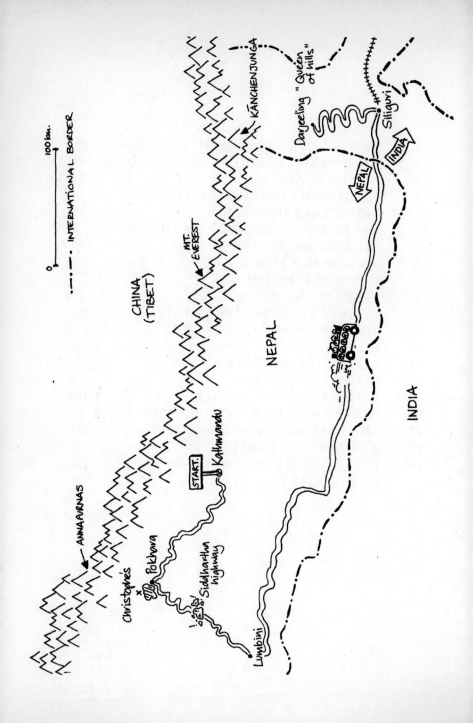

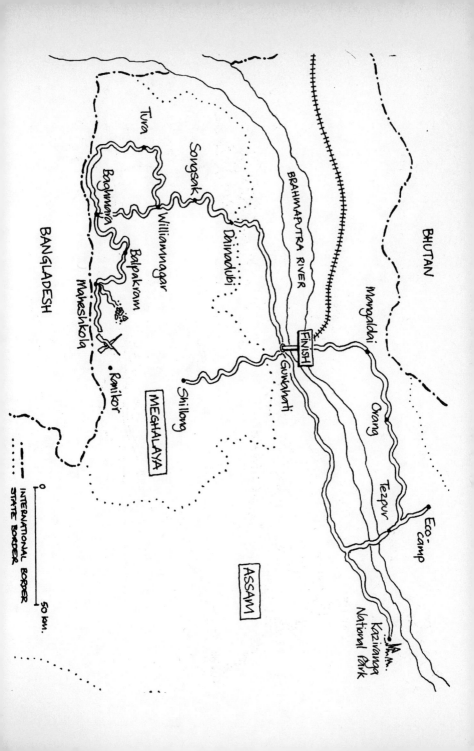

1

SWANS, LOVE AND TOMATO CONCASSE

It was my fourth audition in a row and the calibre of dance company I was auditioning for was becoming steadily more suspect. I had managed to convince myself that a job with the Christian Dance Company, performing in churches in southeast London, was at least a job where I would be dancing. I pinned my number on the front of my leotard and entered the studio. One look at the happy-clapper guitarist strumming away in the corner, one quick glance at the choreographer telling everyone to be 'happy and free' and I turned on my heels and left the room.

I walked home with a heart as heavy as lead trying to stop the negative dialogue running through my head. 'I'm not good enough. I need to do more training. I'm not fit enough. I'm too fat. I'm too thin ... Tomorrow I will start again. No, tomorrow I quit.' Tomorrow came and I rummaged in my purse for the last few pounds to spend on doing a class. The first few minutes are always depressing until that magic happens when body and music join together bringing with it such intense joy that it inhabits every cell, every nerve-ending leaving me with no doubt as to what to do. There is no other option but to carry on. This is what I am. I am Polly and I dance.

At the age of nineteen I joined the Northern Ballet Theatre under the directorship of the late Christopher Gable. For the first year I euphorically traipsed the country dancing the role of the girlfriend of the third Spear Carrier on the left. In my second year I was allowed to venture out onto the proscenium arch and by my third year I was promoted to Soloist. My roles now had a name and my dressing room was nearer the stage.

For the next two years I worked myself to the bone, slowly beginning to trust in my artistic capabilities and longing for the day when I would be made Principal Ballerina. But then an unaccountable thing happened: I began to have suspicions that perhaps there was more to life than being a fairy, a swan or a woodland nymph at 7.30 every night. I began to dread going on tour; another theatre, another town with a faceless shopping precinct, another twenty-four hours spent in suffocating proximity to the same thirty people.

I finally plucked up the courage to tell Christopher Gable that I was leaving the safety of the company to boldly go out into the world of freelance dancing. He was never very good at letting go of his dancers and with me he was no exception. Far from encouraging me, he painted a picture of rejection, financial instability and panic.

Undeterred and full of confidence I came down to London, exchanged my pointe shoes for baggy tracksuit pants and tentatively stepped into the world of contemporary dance. My confidence began to wane as his words of warning rang true.

Although dance is common ground, dancers from different fields eye each other with undisguised caution. Ballet dancers are derisively called 'Bun-heads' and Contemporary dancers are thought never to have seen a Lady Shaver in their lives. Eventually, after cutting my hair and refraining from waxing my legs, I was accepted into their circles and got a job with a company called Dance Theatre Red. It was creative and experimental and I loved it.

Gone were the barn-like Opera Houses of Manchester and Saddlers Wells, gone were the sponsorship hospitality evenings. No longer did I have to schmooze with the heads of major British companies, my recent exertion still shining on my face, whilst trying to look every part the graceful ballerina as I knocked back a vodka and tonic and tried not to eat a chicken vol-au-vent too greedily. The comments were always the same, 'Gosh, I didn't think ballet dancers ate! Look, and you're smoking!' I always responded in the same way too, a fixed smile and a little 'aren't I naughty' shrug of the shoulders.

With Dance Theatre Red our rehearsal rooms were wherever we could find cheap and appropriate space; The Buddhist Arts Centre in Bethnal Green or a converted mill deep in a Gloucestershire village. I lived in digs with a lesbian Installation Artist and a black Labrador called Plank. Unfortunately with this type of dance money is not abundant, every penny is accounted for and weekends are often given up for extra rehearsals. We were very much at the hands of the Arts Council and other funding bodies who, on a whim, could cut our grant by half not realising the serious ramifications that followed.

A yearly schedule would go like this: work for three months then two months off, work for four months then three months off, and so on. It was exhausting and unsettling. The day after a contract ended I would have to find work immediately to keep paying the bills. Sometimes it would be other dancing contracts, other times waitressing, secretarial work, teaching, washing-up or leafleting. They should coin a phrase for the likes of me, 'Jack of all trades and master of one.' On a good day I would feel bohemian, on a bad day just plain pissed-off!

It was during one of my waitressing stints that I met Tim, a beautiful, cheeky, Dutch/Kiwi chef. I remember the day well; I had been dancing abroad and had not worked in the restaurant for a few months. I entered the kitchen whereupon a chef, whom I had never seen before, looked up, put down his knife and walked straight over to me. Amidst the clamour of the kitchen he engaged me in conversation ignoring the orders from the head chef to get back to his prepping. I couldn't help but admire his gall, he enchanted me immediately.

A few weeks passed and we became more and more aware of each other. He would turn the ingredients for the pasta of the day into

11

a concasse of hidden agendas and woo my taste buds by adding something special to my staff dinner. One night he seduced me in the storeroom beside a box of oyster mushrooms and a crate of baby leeks.

From the start I had always known that Tim would have to go back to New Zealand if he wanted to keep his permanent resident status, but I regarded this as my 'get-out' clause. Forewarnings of being left a visa widow didn't concern me: Tim, you see, never fitted into my picture of the ideal man. He is five years younger than me, an Antipodean with spurious traits from the Low Countries and always accompanied with a pervading aroma of garlic and chilli. I had been brought up to mate with the bigger-older-stronger archetype.

But in life, ideals are always challenged and no one was more surprised than me when I realised I had fallen in love with him as I took his Butternut Tortes to table twelve.

Before returning home Tim was going to fulfil his life-long dream of cycling around India with his friend Lee. This didn't come as much of a surprise. From the age of seven he had spent his summer holidays cycling across Holland and Belgium. The preparations for the trip were all-consuming but, although I coo-ed over his made-to-measure bike and organised the shipping company to come and collect his belongings, I remained removed and distant. He was about to embark on something that I could never conceive of doing and his spirit of adventure made me love him all the more.

And so it was that one month before his departure date I came home from another failed audition, the river of disappointment now running a little deeper into my heart. Tim picked his moment well; through my tears he took hold of my face, 'Come with me?' he said.

I didn't answer him. 'Come with me?'

A torrent of ifs and buts tumbled from my mouth, '…but my dancing?'

'What dancing? You have no dancing at the moment.'

'But that still doesn't mean I can come with you, I'm not that sort, I don't do adventure like you do.'

Not for a moment had I ever associated myself with the pioneering echelons of the worldly-wise travellers. They seem to be a different breed far removed from the world I occupy. Adventurous travel to my mind comes hand in hand with sickness, horrors and tests of character. I have always been rather scared and harbour the belief that my neurotic streak would have a chance to live out its full potential. The more I banged out the reasons why I couldn't go the more Tim assured me that this was exactly what I needed to do. I told him I would give him the answer in a week.

For three days I went through every argument as to why I shouldn't go with him but with each rationale my seed of excitement grew. There seemed to be not one good reason for staying behind. I tried to imagine saying goodbye to Tim on my doorstep on what would inevitably be a wet, bleak January day in London.

I tried to imagine kissing him for the final time, then shutting the door and going through the motions of getting ready for my day. Coming home to an empty house, imagining Tim weaving his way through the streets of Kathmandu, wondering if we would ever see each other again. And then what? Weeks of waiting patiently to see what our love amounted to, to see if it was the 'real thing' or if it was only intense but insubstantial.

What if I could use this trip as a test of love? If we still loved each other at the end then I would know to go with him to New Zealand. I wanted to see if Tim would still love me sweating and bitching up a mountain, unwashed and unkempt and out of my depth. But what about him? What was to say that my gentle Tim wouldn't turn into a testosterone-fuelled monster? I wanted to see how we were in all possible circumstances before I made the decision to go and live with him on the other side of the world.

I didn't think I was being overly cautious, just a little extreme perhaps. My friends tried to take the edge off.

'Couldn't you at least go on motorbikes?'

'I'm sure a couple of weeks of cycling in Scotland would give you a pretty good idea.'

No! It was this or nothing.

We were to start our journey in Nepal, joining the hundreds of Indian and Chinese bicycles in the hubbub of Kathmandu. After cycling through the foothills of the Himalayas and around the Kathmandu Valley we were to cross the Indian border at Kakarbhitta and cycle up to the hill station of Darjeeling. From there crossing West Bengal and the North Indian plains into the region least visited by foreigners: Assam and Meghalaya.

Assam has been closed to visitors for the last twenty years: bombings, kidnappings, murders, detonated express trains and blown-up bridges have been commonplace occurrences in the still unresolved pursuit for independence. Although it has now been declared safe for visitors the Government's Unified Command is still firmly installed to counter any insurrectionary operations.

So why were we going to such an unsavoury place? A friend of Lee's, a man called Finn who specialises in remote cycling tours, discovered the uniqueness of this part of India a few years before. He came back consumed with the unspoiled beauty of the place and urged us to go before the Coca-Cola signs are brandished and the backpacking trail firmly entrenched.

I harassed every sales person in countless bookshops to find some travel literature on Assam but nothing came up apart from the skinniest chapter in *Lonely Planet*. It was becoming clearer by the day that we were going to uncharted territory. I tried to keep my nerves under control but they inched their way out and wriggled around my chest catching me unawares. The more stories we heard from Finn about tribal pygmies and headhunters the more I wanted to back out. But with each bout of nerves I had an equal amount of resolve; I was going to do this and that was that.

There was no time to get fit, in the cycling sense. I just had to hope that sheer determination would hold me up until my stamina and muscle power kicked in. I was worried about being a woman on such an expedition, hoping that I wouldn't hamper their progress by issues like menstrual cycles or cycle maintenance.

We spent many hours at Lee's flat writing endless lists of vital equipment. Lee has to be one of the most organised people I know; it is not enough for him to do a one-stop bonanza at Cotswold Outdoor like I did. As I looked at his carefully researched cycling gear, all slim-fit, waterproof, air-venting and micro-fibre with a recurring colour theme of lilac, I felt the first attack of nerves.

We left just after Christmas and the New Year, surviving one set of absurdities to embark upon another. For the week leading up to our departure strange things started happening to me; I came out in a curious rash on my face and developed an angina-like spasm around my heart. People suddenly felt duty-bound to tell me of their near fatal diseases caught in India, tales of lying in a two-bit hospital losing consciousness and all belongings. Lee was struck down with bad flu and he looked like he was at death's door before we had even arrived.

I inoculated myself to the eyeballs, put together a first aid kit worthy of treating war casualties and purposely bypassed the audition page in *The Stage*. The winds of adventure had started blowing; all I had to do was ride.

'He that is a traveller must have the back of an ass to bear all,

a tongue like the wagging of a dog to flatter all,

the mouth of a hog to eat what is set before him,

the ear of a merchant to hear all and say nothing.'

Thomas Nashe
1567 - 1601

2
KATHMANDU, I'LL SOON BE SEEING YOU

Sitting in the plane I opened my guide book and read for the hundredth time "Abode of the Gods", "Roof of the World", "Birthplace of Buddha and residence of some of the most eminent Hindu deities." I don't think I had ever heard such a thrilling set of epithets. I read on, my tongue tripping over the words.

> "......Nepal, a country that is hardly bigger than
> England and Wales and yet boasts eight out of the
> world's ten highest mountains. Rivers wend their way
> from the loftiest of mountaintops to tropical jungle;
> sherpas tend their yaks in the mountain shadows
> whilst thousands of feet below elephants and rhinos
> lumber across the emerald plains of the Terai."

My mind was working faster than a flicker book. I was finding it hard to resist flinging open my arms and shouting 'Take me there!' at the top of my lungs. I was anticipating cycling through an adventure playground, a thrill-a-minute that would challenge and transcend me from the mindset of my city lifestyle.

But first Kathmandu beckoned. I had been warned that I would be disappointed, that the laconic strumming of Cat Stevens paints a much more glamorous picture than the reality of pollution, filth and hassle. Well, they were wrong. I couldn't even say the name without a bodysuit of goose pimples spreading from my head to my toes. Kathmandu, such a pleasing, rhythmic word to say.

We arrived late at night on the last plane out from Delhi. Thank God for sherpas, although the fee they demanded was enough to keep us fed and watered for two days. As long as they touched our belongings at some point they deemed themselves eligible for some hefty remuneration.

We booked into the Kathmandu Guesthouse, a gracious colonial building with open fires and wood panelling that lulled us into a false sense of luxury. It was in these gardens that a friend first got stoned ten years ago. Gazing at the stone Buddha statues dotted around the garden and the huge grapefruits dangling from the trees it was easy to believe that this was a venue for many a personal historic event.

The plan was to stay in Kathmandu a few days in order to become acclimatised to being in a third-world country. It doesn't matter how many books and pictures you might have looked at, nothing can prepare you for the shock of experiencing squalor and poverty at such close quarters.

I felt myself doing everything very gingerly during those first few days. I sipped at my tea waiting for the first grip of stomach cramps; I walked the streets with my arms wrapped tightly around me; I gave my fork an added clean under the table with my napkin hoping that Lee and Tim wouldn't catch me doing so.

Two steps from the Guesthouse and we were in the main thoroughfare of central Thamel, the hub of the tourist district. Even in one of the more spiritual and supposedly immaterial places on earth the power of shopping must not be underestimated. Just imagine an exotic Camden Market where the shoppers were just as stoned and equally dreadlocked.

Yak wool sweaters, Gurkha knives and spiritual bookshops were plentiful, as were the bars with cringing names such as *The Enlightened Yak*, *Cosmic Café* and *Bar Nirvana*. This slightly dampened my spirits; my naïve hope to come to a place infused with a spiritual incandescence already made a mockery by the tidal wave of western commercialism.

One morning as we were walking around the narrow streets of Derber Square, trying not to fall foul of kamikaze rickshaws or trip over sleeping cows, a voice piped up behind us. He tugged at Lee's sleeve,

'Please sir, may I have your gogs (sunglasses) sir? I love your gogs.'

'Thank you but I need them myself.'

'Please sir, if you give them to me then my girlfriend will marry me and I will have good fortune all my days.'

He stayed with us for an hour keeping up a running dialogue as to why Lee's sunglasses would be beneficial to him. I had to marvel at his tenacity although the desire to shake his shoulders and bellow 'NO' was quite overwhelming.

'Just tell me yes or no and I go from here.'

'No, and please leave us alone now.'

'But sir, my girlfriend will not marry me. Please sir, you do not want me to have bad life?'

I felt that I should warn him; once the novelty of the sunglasses wears off she will want him in Calvin Klein's and Levi jeans. He should quit while he's ahead. The only way we got rid of him was by slinking into the murky depths of a handy temple.

Sadly we encountered this obsession with all things western in some form every day. It may have been a half-hour discussion with a travelling Punjabi about the idiosyncrasies of Abba and Boney M, or telling disappointed people we were from England and not from the hallowed land of America.

In the sixties Nepal was known as the Mecca of the Hippies, the abundant flow of hash and ganja helping to magnify the mystic and sublime. Now visitors fall into two camps: the Hippies and the Trippies. There are many tie-dyed dropouts who have had one too many life changing experiences in this land of fantasy. The hassle of applying for

19

housing benefit or the slog of finding a job can surely wait another month? Meanwhile, add one more Buddhist amulet to the neck and continue contemplating life and death over a sweet banana *lassi*.

Then there are the Trippies. This is where I raise my hand; gap-year eighteen year-olds with eyes full of wonder and, 'Hey, amazing man!' never far from their lips; the established professionals who want to put their six-figure salary lifestyles back into perspective; the romantics and enlightenment seekers; the adrenaline bunnies and nature lovers. But we all have one thing in common - a fleece! Polartec prevails. In cafés All-Weather Karrimors jostle against Nike Dry-Fits in a lurid colour explosion. What did we Trippies do before the invention of man-made fibres?

The best way to describe Kathmandu is like being a seven-year old let loose in Disney Land. But in this Disney Land your pocket money never runs out and all the rides you can walk straight on. There are freak shows around every corner to make you suck in your cheeks. In place of Goofy wander semi-naked *Sadhus*, smeared with ash, matted hair and painted faces to have your picture taken with although it probably wouldn't be wise to sit on their knee.

Trying to choose which of the many temples to visit poses the same dilemma as trying to pick which of the January sales to go to. We caught a taxi, our bikes still dismantled, up to Pharping, a heart-stoppingly beautiful part of the Kathmandu Valley. Just out of the village is the Dakshinkali Mandir temple, one of the most sacred of Hindu pilgrimages. Dedicated to the Goddess Kali, "...born of anger, drinker of blood", pilgrims travel miles to perform their ritual slaughter of hapless chickens or, if feeling extravagant, uncastrated, black male goats.

I found it rather ironic that Tim and Lee, two ardent vegetarians, practically ran to the scene of the crime saying with relish, 'I hope we see some killings!' We did. Thankfully they were mercifully quick, one deft swipe across the throats swelling the gutters that already ran with blood. Kali looked greedy too with her multitude of arms and long, pointy tongue.

In contrast to this blood and gore is the Buddhist temple of Swayambhunath. Tradition says that when the Kathmandu Valley was a vast lake, Buddha Vipashyin, an Enlightened One from a previous age, cast a lotus seed into the water. The flower bloomed into a thousand petals and from its centre a hillock rose, the "self-arisen" Swayambhu.

Many years later the Bodhisatva Manjushri, sent from the land of Nirvana to help people find The Truth, severed the lake with his sword creating a gorge. The waters drained, the land became habitable and the hill of the "Lotus Light" accessible for worship. Later, Buddha came here to meditate and preach. Even the hundreds of fluorescent-bottomed monkeys that leapt across my path as I climbed four hundred treacherous steps to pay homage were not your average primates. They are believed to have descended from the lice in Manjushri's hair; as his shorn locks fell to the ground the lice turned into monkeys and each strand of hair into a tree.

I entered the holy complex full of expectation. I had read Herman Hesse's *Siddhartha*, I had been on a retreat and flirted with a good few philosophies in an attempt to make sense of life. Here in Nepal was I going to experience the lifeblood of Buddhism? Was I going to come away committed to saving all sentient beings?

In the middle of the courtyard was a stupa: a white, spherical mound adorned with a thirteen-ring spire, each ring representing the degrees of knowledge needed to attain enlightenment. Buddha's all-seeing, all-knowing eyes were painted below the spire but, not wishing to hear praise of himself, he had no ears nor did he have a mouth for silence is golden.

From the tip of the spire, fanning outwards like a maypole, were garlands of prayer flags. A set of prayer flags always comes in the same sequence symbolising the five elements: blue for space, white for water, red for fire, green for air and yellow for earth. Mantras were inscribed on these "horses of the wind" and when the wind blew each individual blessing scattered to the four corners of the earth. It was beautifully simple unlike the shrine that resembled more of a Blackpool Pier novelty kiosk. How much glitz and gaudiness could they decorate Buddha with? Having spent a lifetime unattaching himself from his ego he was now enshrined with flashing coloured fairy lights, plastic flowers and florid tinsel. It seemed so inappropriate in its felicity.

Recoiling, I stepped out into the courtyard bumping straight into a crocodile of saffron-robed young monks. Authenticity at last perhaps? I watched them spin the prayer wheel and circle the shrine clockwise. I searched their faces for a sign that they were somehow different from us, were their faces more benign, their movements more measured? But as I watched I noticed a couple of them delve into rucksacks and pull out cameras! I then turned my head and behind a stone edifice a group of them were playing footie with a makeshift ball. This was the Nepalese equivalent of a school trip to St. Paul's Cathedral. I went away suppressing a smile at my expectations and assumptions. Lesson number one of the Four Noble Truths of Buddha – do not expect, do not assume. I may have felt disappointed but I couldn't resist backtracking to the prayer wheel to seek a blessing for our journey.

The atmosphere in the streets of Kathmandu intoxicated me. The air vibrated with the smell of wood smoke and esoteric murmuring. On every doorway dog-eared posters advertised Yoga classes, meditation courses and Tantric massage. It was too enticing to pass by. I opted for a Yoga class at the Himalayan Health Centre and dragged Tim along. A whippet of a woman led us into a dimly lit room that looked just like a student 'chill-out' den except this was the real thing - or was it? We were the only participants but there was no going back. It took a while to decipher what she was saying.

'You must have piss.'

Confusion. Maybe she wanted us to go to the loo before we started.

'You can achieve piss by breeding in your nafal aria.'

Aaah, it began to make sense. She guided us through positions whilst we tried hard to unify our minds and bodies through our 'breeding'. Half way through a salute to the sun, whilst passing my heart and stomach chakras along the floor, I felt the first nip, followed by the second, the third, the fourth…Before long my torso was on fire and a surreptitious look confirmed all suspicions: I was covered in bites.

Not wanting to offend our gentle lady by insinuating that her rugs were bug-ridden all I could do was tuck in my layers of T-shirts when she wasn't looking. As I lay face up on the infested rug my concentration was absorbed in figuring out how to 'release the palms of my feet off, relaxing all my tumbs (?)' and thankfully not on the creatures feasting on my body. We finished the lesson with humming 'OM' and drinking tea of freshly ground herbs and spices.

My tranquil, if itchy, state was short-lived. We went back to assemble our bikes only to discover that they had not survived the journey unscathed. Tim's handlebars were irretrievably bent and the rim of my back wheel cracked and warped, the implications of which I was to find out later.

Returning in the evening to the Kathmandu Guesthouse after dining on 'chilly soop' and 'pillow rice and vegitibals,' we relaxed around the fire in the lobby. The comfy chairs housed weary trekkers with weather-beaten faces and a look of accomplishment about them. I felt like a junior looking admiringly at the seniors as they came out of their O'levels. 'One day I'll be that clever', 'One day I'll be that intrepid.' It vexed me slightly that everyone in the Guesthouse was heading upwards on foot whereas we were venturing sideways on two wheels.

The atmosphere on the eve of our departure was tense. Lee was chomping at the bit to be in the saddle; four days in Kathmandu were two days too many. I was suffering from severe anxiety, suddenly crippled with doubt about my physical capabilities. Tim's and Lee's dauntless excitement highlighted my fearfulness. Retorts back home such as, 'You may as well cycle criss-cross up the M1 in the opposite direction,' resounded in my ears. The reactions from our fellow guests were equally disconcerting.

'Cycling? You must be mad!'

'I don't know. Are we?' I replied.

A friendly American who slipped into the 'I used to be an alcoholic gambler until I came to Nepal' category, tried to dispel my fears by telling us a story he had heard a few days before. The event had occurred on the route that we would be taking the following day. A truck was going too fast and knocked down a villager. Word got to the village who quickly put up a blockade. The driver and his mate saw the blockade and the angry villagers and abandoned the truck to run up into the hills. They were chased and killed. The villagers believe that the motor vehicle is spawned from the devil and revenge is ruthless.

Unfortunately this story did little to pacify me, not only are the drivers careless but the villagers barbaric. Great! In my mind God left something out when he created humankind. He was proficient with senses and organs, nerves and limbs but to me he messed up when it came to the brain, which is why computers win hands down over us – they have a selective memory, we do not. How many times have I been told something or overheard something that I categorically do not want to remain in my memory bank? If only we had an icon of a wastepaper basket in the grey matter of our frontal lobe to dump all the negative information that we come across and with a single click it vanishes never to be recalled again. During that evening I heard one thing too many that I knew would stick firmly in my memory.

I went to bed experiencing the same feelings as I did before the First Night of a new ballet. Closing my eyes I would go through all of my steps of the entire three acts obsessing where I could go wrong: a difficult balance in Act One I that I could misjudge, a series of pirouettes in the finale where I could fall over. In truth it rarely happened but often the first grey light of dawn would show in the crack of the curtains before I fell asleep.

"A woman will always sacrifice herself if you give her the opportunity. It is her favourite form of self-indulgence."

W. Somerset Maughan
'The Circle', 1921

3
ON THE ROAD

We got up at the crack of dawn hoping to dodge the morning mayhem of Kathmandu. Togged up to the neck in thermals and with a belly full of porridge we launched ourselves onto the streets. Swerving past a motor-rickshaw on a death mission and rebounding over a series of potholes whilst nearly decapitating a bewildered chicken, I had the alarming discovery of not seeming to possess any back brakes.

I yelled 'STTOOOPPPP!' at the top of my lungs and had a small epileptic fit in front of the men. They patiently explained to me that because my back wheel was warped, if my brakes were tight then the wheel would get stuck. I had to have loose brakes in order to move forward. I was aghast! I was about to embark on a six week journey through some of the hilliest, most potholed terrain in the world on one set of brakes. These were also not that efficient as due to a bent wheel spoke my panniers had to be attached to the front. Between them they did a bit of tweaking and gave me some professional advice.

'Poll, just leave a lot of time before stopping.'

I hadn't planned on using my helmet, mainly because I am vain but also for temperature reasons, but visions of my mother receiving news of my multiple head injuries made me think twice about it. I swallowed hard, took a deep breath and fastened my chinstrap.

The road to Pokhara took us along the Prithvi Highway deep into Gurkha country. The highway is named after the famous Gurkha, King Prithvi Narayan Shah. He was born in 1723 and at the age of twenty succeeded to the Gurkha throne where a saint in disguise told him that he would rule wherever his feet took him (my guess is that Richard Branson was also paid a visit by the same saint). He fulfilled

27

this prophecy by becoming the most influential king that Nepal had ever known. Under his rule he took control of the Tibetan borders and conquered the separate states of the Kathmandu Valley, uniting the Kingdom of Nepal for the first time.

Gurkha translates as 'bravest of the brave'. These stocky, sturdy hillsmen fear nothing and nobody. The way they wield the Gurkha knife has been described as the most fearful sight in military history. In years past it was believed that the long, curved blade could not be returned to its scabbard unless it had been smeared with blood. Now, however, they cut their own fingers in order to satisfy the gods.

The highway was beautiful, when we could see it. Each time a truck rumbled past it belched out a thick, black cloud of fumes that made breathing difficult and obscured the road ahead. We needn't have worried, the volume of their horns alerted us to their presence.

The more the truck was decorated, the hipper the driver. There was definitely some connection with the shrines, metres of the ubiquitous tinsel, flashing Buddhas on the dashboard and a collection of stickers on the windscreen. Alarmingly, some had so many that only the smallest of eye-spaces was left clear for the driver to look through. Not until we had our TTT (Truck Toleration Tactic) worked out - holding our breath and sticking as close to the side of the road as possible - could we begin to enjoy the first step of our journey.

There was so much to take in that it alleviated the pain of spending those first few agonising days in the saddle. If I'm honest it didn't alleviate it enough. Quite a lot of the time I wanted to cry at the mental and physical anguish that I seemed to be suffering.

'It'll get better we promise you,' said Tim and Lee.

There were moments when I believed them but they really only lasted a nano-second. I found myself adhering to a pattern; the first few kilometres of the day were sheer hell until my legs warmed up, and for a couple of hours I cycled along feeling pretty chirpy and pleased with myself. But for the twenty kilometres before lunch it was as if someone had pulled the plug on my resources.

In the time it took for someone to click their fingers my stamina and muscle-power drained from my body. I wasn't even like one of those wind-up toys that gradually peters out, rather more like a CD that suddenly becomes stuck in the same place. No matter how much I pedalled it felt like I was making no progress whatsoever. Lee would carry on, his figure becoming smaller and smaller. Tim would have kept him company but if he still wanted to call me his girlfriend he knew what was best for him.

'Tim! Don't go so fast. How much further till lunch time?'

'Twelve k's, that's all.'

The boys each had one of those computers on their handlebars that tells you your speed, your average speed, the altitude, kilometres cycled and how your shares are doing on the stockmarket. I knew that if I were to have one I would spend every cycling minute checking how far I had ridden; so I didn't - I relied on Tim instead.

'How much further now?'

'Eleven k's and quit your asking, you're driving me nuts.'

Uh oh! Was it starting already? The demise of our rock-solid relationship was being tested after only the second day. I made a rule with myself there and then. I would only ask the distance every half an hour. Surely that wouldn't be too irritating?

At the slightest of inclines I learnt the seriousness of weight. I regretted packing my eye repair gel, emergency moisture surge and extra pair of trousers. Hard-core cycle tourers, so I have been told, drill holes in their spoon, saw the handle off their mug and cut the labels out of clothes in the never-ending quest for a lighter load. I am not that puritanical. There are certain things in life that would be downright careless for a woman to be without, and if it meant popping them into Tim's panniers when he wasn't looking then so be it. I was caught.

'Polly, what are these things in my panniers?'

'I need them. You don't want me ending up a weather-beaten old hag now do you?'

He didn't have an answer for that so there they remained.

The few networks of roads in Nepal were not built until the 1970s and many died in the process. At times the road was tortuous, carved out of sheer rock faces that clung to the mountainside and sliced through rice terraces. Often we had to screech to a halt after speeding round a corner where a landslide had washed away the road. Below us lay ravines and icy rivers, behind us the skid marks of our tyres with the faintest whiff of smoke encircling the rubber. We took a couple of minutes to compose ourselves before carrying on.

Despite newcomer's legs those first few days of cycling were fabulous, our senses drunk on the riot of colour and the hum of life. On either side were thatched mud huts, tumbling streams and terraced smallholdings. Kids waved furiously at us and ran to the side of the road shouting, 'Hello! Goodbye! Chicken burger!'

The old traveller's adage of taking a stash of pens to give to the children is still circulated. They repeated like a mantra, 'Please sir, pen sir!'

The difference now is that they don't need them, their top pockets were already home to four shiny pens of their own.

In practically every village there was a group of budding entrepreneurs. The young horrors set up road tolls of their own using a piece of string. Their little hands held steadfastly to each end, a metre above the road. As we came to a hasty stop nearly catapulting ourselves over the string, they would pounce on us demanding rupees. If we were not forthcoming they dived across our panniers making it impossible to cycle off.

Other times we had stones thrown at our wheels and kids running for all their might beside us, screaming at the top of their lungs. It was never vindictive, they were just full of energy and mischief.

The villages we cycled through were swollen with people; toddlers clambering over grandfathers, school kids with baby sisters in slings across their backs, aunts admonishing teenagers, mothers chivvying goats and men lolling in the sunshine. The majority were smiling, the majority looked well fed and the majority were filthy.

Personal ablutions took place in rivers or under roadside pipes that trickled down icy Himalayan water. The colour of our skin made the women coyly cover their breasts, suspended in motion, whilst large chocolate eyes followed our progression.

It is true, cows are holy. They looked like they knew it too. Amidst the chaos the beasts basked in the sunshine, noses lifted slightly in the air, eyes semi-closed with an adopted air of superiority. Most of the population of Nepal are Newars who are descended from the Mongols; they make every day a celebration of life and death and once a year honour one of the family cows. To them the cow personifies Lakshmi, the Goddess of Wealth, and in order to bring prosperity to the family the cow must be treated to feasts of rice and grain.

Never have I seen so much faeces, both human and animal; the dogs were not discerning however, they licked either. I felt consumed by it; if I wasn't sidestepping it then I was smelling it, talking about it, not doing it or doing it too much. Loo paper became a prized commodity in which Lee held all the shares; he had cycled around Burma and knew to bring his own supply. After Tim's and my one pack of Handy Andys had run out and we had recycled a tatty napkin from Costa Coffee at Heathrow we were at the mercy of Lee's generosity. Never again will I travel without a little box of that tissue paper kind that never seems to run out. There is something rather demeaning about having to ask for loo paper especially if you're given one sheet and you think you might actually need two.

It took us two days and then a pitch-black ride to reach the strange town of Pokhara. Until thirty years ago the place hardly existed but with the growing demands of trekkers and hippies the town soon burgeoned. Pokhara lies on the shores of Lake Phewa in whose waters the silhouettes of the Annapurnas are reflected. So far I hadn't seen so much as a glimpse of the Himalayas; I was beginning to get impatient.

Several kilometres before reaching Pokhara we stopped for a tea break at a roadside shack. As we sipped our tea and rested our quivering legs we watched a scruffy motorbike splutter to a stop beside our bikes, cocooning them in a cloud of dust. An even scruffier character dismounted and came and sat down beside us.

Christophe was a Frenchman who arrived in Nepal twenty-five years ago; he fell in love with a local lady followed by the local herb, or he fell in love first with the local herb and then with a local lady (I think with Christophe they are one and the same), and married her. They had a number of kids and a guesthouse. His commitment to making a living out of tourists' purses was as urgent as any Nepali and he wasted no time in giving us the hard sell; we promised we would stay with him.

Pokhara was the town that never came. With each supposed last kilometre we would come across another signpost informing us we still had five more to go. To a person who has never ridden a bike with all manner of items attached to it that short distance might appear insignificant. Not so, even a miscalculated one hundred metres is like walking home from the supermarket laden down with shopping and realising you left your purse at the checkout.

The frustration and exhaustion was overwhelming, waves of nausea engulfed me and I had to squeeze back the tears so as not to appear feeble. To help ease the pain I invented a mental visualisation game to make the kilometres go quicker. I knew that it was five kilometres from my house to my friend Kate's and back again. I have cycled this route seven million times and it is no distance at all. As I cycled along the road to Pokhara I visualised I was turning out of Cranbrook Road, cycling past the Kebab shop on the corner, over the zebra-crossing in front of Blockbuster Video and then turning into Acton Lane. I was half-way there.

'Tim, how much further?' (I hadn't asked for at least forty-five minutes).

'Two kilometres, three at the most.'

All I had to do now was reverse the journey and we would be in Pokhara.

It worked, although Pokhara at night was not so inviting as Chiswick. When we finally arrived we found the town shrouded in darkness and eerily quiet. By the flickering light of a kerosene lamp we tried to figure out Christophe's map. Every time we stopped a figure materialised from out of nowhere like a hologram, 'Heh, my uncle has very nice hotel, please you come with me.'

The voice dropped in volume. 'You want smoke?'

We turned off down a dirt track that took us along the lakeside but the gradual thinning of civilisation made us even more on edge. Just as we were beginning to think we would have to take a chance with a drug-dealing landlord a little voice rang out in the darkness.

'Are you looking for my Daddy?'

It was the voice of an angel. She took us through a gate into a garden where Christophe was holding court around a fire, toking on an enormous joint. With eyes that looked like red crazy paving he made everyone make room for us and we collapsed beside the fire. Through the course of the evening people came and went, sitting down to weave stories of the mountains and prodding absent-mindedly at the fire. Christophe had obviously started a trend, his wife's sisters and cousins had also married Frenchmen. I tried to join in with the erratic threads of conversation but it all proved too much for me. I put my head down. I was lulled into contentment by the soft chuckling around me, the smell of wood smoke and the twinkling stars above. So this was Pokhara. Hmmm, I hoped we would stay a while.

We were woken by the noise of an early morning chain gang passing platters of stones up to a nearby roof. Our room at Christophe's was more like a cell; the only furniture was a bed which had curious stool pellets resting on the pillow, even in sleep there was no guarantee of a respite from faeces. At eighty pence a night we couldn't complain. In the morning the beauty of Pokhara revealed itself in all its glory. From the viewpoint of our rickety balcony we could see the diamond-studded waters of the lake and behind us the peaks of the Annapurnas and Machhapuchhere. Words cannot describe the awesome beauty of these mountains so I shall tell a story instead.

Next to Annapurnas I, II, III and IV and beside Dhaulagiri lies Machhapuchhere, otherwise known as the 'Fishtail Mountain.' It is heralded as the most beautiful mountain in the world because of the perfect symmetry of its twin peaks. An expedition tried to conquer it in the early 1950s but five hundred metres before reaching the summit they had to turn back; the jaggedness of the Fishtail's slopes made it impossible for them to continue. On their descent they told the locals that at least one mountain should remain unconquered in veneration to its divine beauty. To this day the mountain stands undefiled by humankind.

One of the great things about staying with Christophe was his chef Siva, another saint in disguise, put on this earth to fill the bellies of hungry cyclists. Cycling makes you ravenous and you can eat as much as you like, as often as you like. Porridge, eggs, rice and dahl, packets of biscuits (and I'm talking three packets a day) plus loaves of bread which we wolfed down guiltlessly.

My career as a ballet dancer had obviously been figure-orientated although I managed to get through it without too much pain and obsession. I did however live in fear of Monday mornings from the ages of sixteen to nineteen. At my ballet school they employed the barbaric system of weighing the students every week, the girl students that is. Our individual weights would then be read out in front of the class and if they weren't satisfactory we were not allowed to continue training until we had lost or gained the appropriate amount.

As if this wasn't bad enough they chose Monday as the day of reckoning; at least by Wednesday we had jumped, twisted and stretched away the weekend's excesses. For years I associated Sunday night with bowls of All-Bran and hot water, eaten for obvious efficacious reasons! After the hideous ordeal was over we would traipse down to the local 'naff caff' and gorge ourselves with egg and chips and hot chocolate.

I also remember being hauled into the director's office on a charge of smoking in the dressing room. In the middle of my telling-off, the harridan became personal.

'And while we are about it Polly, you will never get a job with a classical ballet company because you don't have any cheekbones.'

To this day I have never felt so mortified, to me it was the cruellest thing one could say to a still self-conscious teenager. Now, when I look back to the photos of my first year with the Northern Ballet Theatre, I wince at my over-accentuated blusher.

We stayed in Pokhara for a couple of days enjoying gazing at the mountains and the lake for hours on end as the gentle rhythm of Christophe and his family went on around us. Yet we couldn't ignore the pull of the mountains; the momentous presence of them was not enough, we felt compelled to ascend. Christophe urged us to go up to Sarangkot, a tiny mountain village that lies at 1,600 metres, to watch the sun sink behind the Annapurnas. He assured us it was only a two hour climb.

Five hours later with calves pumped up enough to challenge Mr Universe we eventually made it to the top just as the sun was setting. The jagged peaks of the mountains were ablaze with golden light. It was the most glorious sight I have ever ever seen. We watched in silent awe as the last rays of sun caressed their flanks before tearing ourselves away for fear of catching hypothermia.

It would be so easy to live like a king in Nepal; a big, fat, lazy, slob of a king eating way too much food and smoking unhealthy amounts of hashish, just about making it to have a massage every day, the rest of the time spent chilling out by the lake. Self-motivation and self-esteem leaving your body as quick as you can say 'I want pancakes and a sweet banana *lassi* please' just because everything is so darn cheap. I went to have a massage in a hut down the path from Christophe's. Before I had even had the first I was planning how many I could fit in before our departure the next day. I had a good excuse for such over-indulgence, I was in desperate need of getting a semblance of normality back into my legs.

As I laid my semi-naked body down onto a grimy pallet I hoped I was not going to be feasted upon again. For an hour I was pummelled and kneaded luxuriating in the swish of her sari as it brushed against my legs and the jangle of her bracelets. Unfortunately, the ill-fitting door could not keep out the Himalayan night air for long and I left more a frozen corpse than a languid sybarite.

Although we had our route planned it is not until you are in the country that you can tell what is possible and what is not. We spent hours poring over maps and doing furious calculations: kilometres versus number of mountain passes, weight of traffic versus condition of the roads. Agreeing on the next leg of our journey ruffled our feathers. We each had different objectives but not the time to satisfy them all. Our different characters were beginning to surface. Lee is more fastidious than Tim and me; he goes through every detail thoroughly before making any decision. Because of his mental application he often assumed that his way was best. I am the complete opposite, led purely by instincts and desires which must have appeared whimsical and rather flaky to Lee.

"Man's main task in life is to give birth to himself"

Erich Fromm

4

SIDDHARTHA HIGHWAY TO LUMBINI, BIRTHPLACE OF BUDDHA

There has never been a more perfect name for a road than the Siddhartha Highway. Not only is the way high but it embodies the teachings of Buddha more than prostrating in front of any shrine. No one is sure why it is called the Siddhartha Highway, perhaps because it finishes near Lumbini, the birthplace of Buddha, or that he travelled through these hills on his way to Kathmandu.

It took us three days of hard cycling from the crack of dawn to late afternoon. Some stretches one could barely call a road, more a mish-mash of different surfaces snaking its way up into the Churia Hills. Just when we thought the road could not become any steeper it shot up another four hundred metres; just when we thought our spines could not withstand another kilometre of juddering the road turned into a dust bowl and we had to dismount and push, and just when it seemed that it could not possibly become more beautiful a family of monkeys swung out in front of us.

Under these conditions I didn't know if it was my body feeling pain or my mind. Buddha teaches that one should commit oneself entirely to the present, not projecting into the future or clinging to the past. He would have accepted that the going was hard but in that hardness things were perfect just the way they were. As the dusty road wove through the hills with the Annapurnas on our right occupying the horizon like a pattern on a milk carton, I tried to commit myself to each passing minute. I wanted to scream out a constant flow of expletives, but I didn't because I knew that wouldn't help. I wanted my bicycle to be equipped with a James Bond device that, with an extra tap on my pedal a motor would kick-start into action and two small wings shoot out from my handlebars and propel me effortlessly onwards. I could fantasise but I knew that wasn't going to get me to the top either. The Siddhartha Highway, it seemed, was teaching me two things: endurance and acceptance, not on a physical level so much as mentally.

It didn't help our spirits when we discovered that our map was fifty kilometres out. In a car that's an extra hour or so, on a bicycle on rough roads that amounts to another whole day. It was getting dark so we made our way to the nearest village to find somewhere to stay. Being a naturally selective sort, I was appointed 'Quality Controller'. There wasn't really much to choose from and so we had to make do with a room with mildew on the walls and the river as a bathroom. Just as we set out to eat the lights in the village fizzled out and we were plunged into darkness much the same as in Pokhara. Electric lights and fresh paint seemed to evade us on a regular basis.

I woke up in the middle of the night certain that someone was trying to pinch our bicycles; it was only a man going outside to cough up his lungs. I couldn't go back to sleep, my heart was thumping and it felt as if a dozen butterflies were trapped in my chest. I didn't know if this was the adverse effect of taking anti-malarial pills or if I was dipping into my constant well of anxiety.

Shortly after leaving the Northern Ballet Theatre I started to suffer from crippling panic attacks. The reasons then were very clear but as the months and years moved on and the attacks were still as strong I thought the reasons must run deeper. I know there are hundreds like me who seemingly have no control over our minds and bodies, distrusting ourselves to do the most mundane of things. For three years I was conscious of every breath I took and every breath felt like it was being dragged through a muslin cloth to get into my lungs. I was petrified of staying a night alone in the house or getting on the tube and yet I could fly to Tokyo to dance in front of hundreds of people. There seemed to be no logic. I now think these attacks are caused by passion, a body full of energy that has no outlet, a fist of unfulfillment lodged in my solar plexus.

In my distress I was desperate to seek platitudes and solutions and I think I must have tried them all. But I hadn't tried cycling through Nepal and India. If people have a phobia then one school of thought is to confront them with the very thing that they fear. If people are scared of heights then make them walk over the top of Sydney Harbour Bridge; afraid of spiders then put them in a room with a dozen of the variety they used in Arachnophobia – the really hairy, sturdy ones. This may be harsh but in my view is the most effective.

My phobia was being in remote places far from civilisation and a hospital. A hospital? Yes, a hospital. Perhaps I have my own phobia unique only to me – farfromhospitalitis – or maybe it comes under the same umbrella as hypochondria. My phobia started after my first panic attack when I thought I was experiencing heart failure that undoubtedly was going to lead to my sudden death. I just about managed to call the ambulance and open my front door before collapsing on the floor begging for my redemption, a hospital and a life support machine. The paramedics arrived but instead of rigging me up to drips and oxygen masks they gave me a very unglamorous brown paper bag instead.

So I kept a paper bag folded up in my purse for two years until one day in the grips of another attack I pulled it out to find that a leaked Ribena carton and a pen hole had rendered its restorative properties useless. I did away with paper bags but my fixation on hospitals still festered. In every new place I went to I would find myself subconsciously clocking the hospital and its distance from where I was staying just in case I should have another attack and this time finally keel over and suffocate.

Here I was awake in the dead of night in some village midway between the Annapurnas and the emerald forests of the Terai. I calculated the nearest hospital to be back in Kathmandu. I listened to the rhythm of Tim's and Lee's breathing as they slept and tried to measure mine the same as theirs. I wasn't going to suffocate, I couldn't suffocate, the hospital was five days ride away. I put my hands to my chest and snuggled closer to Tim. Everything was alright, there was nothing to panic about. As Buddha would have said: things are perfect just the way they are.

I loved early mornings on the road. Even tender buttocks and sleep-sluggish legs made me feel alive and I found I couldn't wait to get out there and see what new treasures lay ahead. The mornings were cold as we cycled along deep ravines full of swirling mist. It was as if the landscape was flirting with us, allowing us just a glimpse of a rice terrace through the clouds or a mountainside of rhododendron bushes illuminated by a shaft of sunlight.

But, if I loved the cycling, then I loved our tea breaks even more. We felt we were sitting in the front row of the cabaret of life, each village having its own cast of different stars. On the way to Tanzen we witnessed 'Spinning-Top Meister.' A boy launched his top into a tornado spin then nonchalantly threw down the string in a circle around the base, with one quick tug the top sprung into the air and landed, still spinning, on the palm of his hand. Tim, always one to rise to a challenge, got out his yo-yo to try and impress the boy and the village with some of his tricks. The problem was he didn't have any and with each attempt he looked more inept and clumsy. In salute to obvious talent he handed over his yo-yo as a present to the accomplished boy.

At the end of each bumpy day the height of our saddles had dropped by inches. I felt my ovaries had jumped into my chest, my kidneys juddered down to sit beside my colon and my intestines lassoed

42

around my heart. I earned myself a song from Tim:

> *'There once was a girl from Farnham Royal*
> *Who cycled the hills of Nepal.*
> *She said, "Hell, these are high"*
> *But she never did cry*
> *And now she's tougher than all!'*

The Siddhartha Highway finally peaked and we revelled in freewheeling down from the mountains. As we entered Butwal on our way to Lumbini and the Sacred Garden where Buddha was born, we hit a wall of mist and gale force winds. The road turned pancake-flat but at the expense of beauty. The town was ugly and depressing, the sky had become grey and overcast and it was bitterly, bitterly cold. We may as well have been slapped in the face. I was already mourning my mountains and the smiling, colourful people.

In this part of Nepal, so close to the border, there are as many Indians as there are Nepalese. The road was three lanes thick on either side with bicycles. I shall always remember the clanking noise of those solid machines carrying labourers and their work tools home from the fields; it seemed that even the bicycles were whimpering in the ghostly air. I felt embarrassed on my sophisticated wheels, our brightly coloured jackets and warm gloves twisting the nail of privilege even deeper into their sides. They were riding wrapped in thin blankets with their skeletal faces peeping out. They looked like the Grim Reaper's offspring. The atmosphere reeked of desperation, no solid buildings, only refugee-like tents fighting to stave off the cold. They couldn't give a damn that just up the road lay the most sacred of places, the birthplace of the Lord Buddha; how could they when it was certain that some would not survive the winter? I vehemently wished we hadn't made this pilgrimage, it felt empty and false. I cycled the last few kilometres to the Sacred Garden with my head down and my feet now completely numb with cold.

We checked in to the only hotel in the area, the Lord Buddha Hotel (novel name). We were the only guests. Tim and I clung together under the paltry drips of a shower. Nothing, it seemed, could get me warm; the sight of the people had put a chill in my heart. We had supper and then went outside to huddle around the fire with the owner of the hotel and the few members of staff. I like the fact that a source of warmth unifies all that sit around it. We sat for a long time listening to the chanting from the monastery through the trees, mesmerised by the flames as chilled dew settled all around.

Siddhartha Gautama Buddha was born in 563 BC. Queen Maya Devi was on her way home to her mother when she went into labour. Some myths say she had a dream in which a white elephant descended from heaven holding a silver lotus in his trunk, others say that a full moon floated down and landed in her lap. It was the first full moon of the lunar calendar and stifling hot. A grove of sal and mango trees provided the shade and she washed in a nearby pool. Upon his birth the baby is said to have taken seven steps in each of the four directions, proclaiming "This is my final re-birth." The earth quaked, flowers fell from the heavens and a host of gods came down to worship him. He was born with thirty-two marks of perfection on his body and the priests declared him destined for greatness.

His mother died shortly afterwards. He was brought up in a palace twenty-four kilometres from Lumbini. He got married and had a son but never once set foot outside the palace grounds until, at the age of twenty-nine he persuaded his consort to show him the nearby countryside. He was so appalled at what he saw that his heart felt like it had been broken in two. The story says that he awoke feeling "like a man who was told his house was on fire." Without saying goodbye to his family he left. He exchanged his fine clothes for the rags of a beggar and renounced all worldly goods.

For six years he wandered, following spiritual gurus and depriving his body of all but what would keep him alive. He wanted to learn the truth of existence but nothing led him closer. In the depths of his despondency he went to Bodh Gaya where he vowed not to move until he had found enlightenment. He meditated beneath a peepul tree withstanding the temptations of the devil who sent his seductive daughters to entice him. He sat in his trance for an entire day and night until he had a vision of an endless cycle of birth and death - the destiny of all men. Buddha had at last found Nirvana.

He carried on his travels preaching the Four Noble Truths and living by the Eighth Fold Path. He taught that life is painful because nothing in this material world is permanent or reliable; suffering is caused by desire, attachment and ignorance. But there is a state beyond this suffering which is called Nirvana - neither being nor not being - which can be reached through living by certain precepts: right understanding, right mindfulness, effort, speech, thought.

It has been said that he had a jealous cousin, Devadutta, who wanted to destroy Buddha and everything that he stood for. By this time Buddha had accumulated a growing number of disciples, one of whom was his son. During one of his sermons Devadutta pushed a large boulder from a peak above but before it had a chance to kill Buddha it split in two with each piece falling either side.

Another story involved a wild elephant that was set loose on Buddha's path. Inches before trampling him the elephant stopped in his tracks, sat down and listened, sensing that his message was for all living beings. Buddha died at the age of eighty; he was cremated and his ashes divided out amongst his disciples. His last words were directed to his favourite disciple, Ananda.

"A Buddha can only point the way. Become a lamp unto yourself. Work out your own salvation diligently."

We walked around the grounds where Buddha was born in the dank, cold morning mist, drops of dew falling on our faces. I entered the temple with slight trepidation but thankfully his flashing aura was slightly more muted this time. As I wandered I tried to feel something special but couldn't quite muster the feeling. We stopped at the holy pillar, our attention caught by some chanting. At the head of the gathering was a shaven monk with a striking profile. Behind him stood a huddle of fat-cat Thais with a 'Super 8' camera; they were making a documentary.

The chanting stopped and the monk turned round to face us – his serious expression suddenly broke into a dazzling, one hundred and eighty watt smile that totally encompassed his face. It was so unexpected that we were taken aback; he lit up the gloomy garden like a flare. He was shivering more than the dog that was quivering at Tim's feet with imploring eyes. All three of us were rooted to the spot, mesmerised by his beauty. We could not seem to tear ourselves away until it became embarrassing and we could think of no reason to linger any longer.

After much deliberation we decided to bypass the long, cold stretch of the Terai by taking a bus. The decision didn't sit well with any of us. We felt it was a bit too soon to take the easy option but we did not have time on our hands as the bad condition of the roads and the incorrect maps had delayed us. If we knew what lay in store then we would not have wasted the energy berating ourselves.

Before boarding the bus we went to get something to eat in a large Victorianesque dining-hall. They knew we were coming, there was a power cut. After a while the lights came on and there adorning the back wall was a 3-D fluorescent picture of a Himalayan gorge, a fishing boat and three birds mid-flight. The beauty of this masterpiece of kitsch was the luminescent lighting of the tranquil scene. It managed to convey the quality of dusk when the sliver of moon first appears.

Lee, a sucker for a still-life photograph, leapt up with relish. Just as his zoom lens protruded - POW! - we were plunged into darkness. He sat down but five minutes later we were rewarded again. All eyes were on the picture as it flickered into glory. Lee jumped up for take number two. By this time we had the full attention of the restaurant that didn't know whether to be apologetic about the state of their electrics or amused by this eccentric white man. This time Lee's finger managed to hover over the button but - POW! The picture came to an abrupt end again. This time they couldn't control their delight; the restaurant erupted into laughter. The third time the lights came on, Lee purposefully left it a few minutes until the atmosphere was so charged that dinners were being left uneaten. He slowly got up; you could hear a pin drop. The lens zoomed out, the finger made it to the button and CLICK, the picture was finally taken. Anyone would have thought he had scored the winning goal of the World Cup, the applause ricocheted around the walls, they were jubilant. We finished our lunch and they came out to say goodbye. The sight of us riding off on our shiny bicycles captivated them even more and we knew that the story of the English man and the picture would be re-lived for years to come.

The bus journey to Kakarbhitta was going to take twelve hours. As we waited for the bus in the early morning we hoped with all our hearts that it would be more in the European vein. When it finally clambered into view a Mexican donkey cart would have had more hope of joining the fleet of National Express. It was a biscuit tin on wheels, cranky, filthy and with no suspension. We lashed our bicycles to the roof with a silent prayer that they would be unloaded in one piece, although I was hoping that my wheel might get bent back into its true position.

Cycling with the extra weight of the panniers on the front was beginning to play havoc with my knees. Every morning I had to cajole them into bending and straightening and no amount of camphor ointments seemed to make a difference. As a dancer I suffered from bad knee injuries and I was starting to suspect that toiling up and down mountains on a bicycle perhaps wasn't the cleverest of things for me to do. There were many occasions when I used to be frightened to go on stage, thinking that my knees wouldn't last the duration of the performance.

Things came to a head one night during a tour of Swan Lake when my courage bottled out. The orchestra started to play the first strains of the overture, I dutifully took my place in the wings behind swan number eleven but, inches before stepping out onto the stage, I froze. It felt like two cleavers were relentlessly sawing through each patella; my knees were on fire and could not be relied upon to withstand landing from even the smallest of jumps. I ran up to the dressing room and furiously started to pack up my belongings. I did not want to have to endure any more pain, I had had enough of dancing. Meanwhile in the auditorium the Ballet Mistress had realised that something was amiss, the lines were lopsided and there were lots of nervous looking dancers wondering how to cover up for the missing swan. She eventually worked out who was missing and came to find me as I was throwing tights and make-up into my bag. She sat me down and talked me into staying. If I gave up because of an injury I would live to regret it for the rest of my life. They were the soundest words of advice I received during my ballet career. After a couple of months off and constant visits to physiotherapists my knees were up and running once more.

Injury was a problem for young dancers whose positions in the

48

company were yet to be fully established. The director hammered it home to us that injuries were a result of a poor technique and we were threatened with losing our jobs if we took too much time off. Yet the workload of rehearsing during the day, then performing every night on various stages, taxed even the most physically blessed of bodies. As a result we would carry on dancing until the injuries became acute and we survived on unhealthy amounts of Nurofen and ice packs. In a perverted way I was quite enjoying my knee pains on this trip. I did not have to perform on them and I was not going to lose my job.

Our friendly booking officer had assured us that the best seats in the bus were in the cabin with the driver. Well maybe he was right if you were the type of person who enjoys death-defying rollercoaster rides and cacophonous horn-tooting. We lasted two minutes and then skulked back to the main body of the bus. Unfortunately I picked the seat that had a tendency to jerk forward every few seconds and my knees bashed rhythmically against the seat in front for the whole twelve hours. The poor woman in front was either suffering from travel sickness (which was doubtful - people here were born to put up with hours of bumpy travel) or she had eaten a dodgy curry the night before. She spat great globs of phlegm at regular intervals that flew past my foot and landed in pools in the middle of the aisle. I watched fascinated as they made their glupey way to the front of the bus.

People got on and off seemingly travelling with half the contents of their house. No valise on wheels here; sparrow-like women heaved huge sacks of rice at the same time as negotiating reams of sari and a couple of kids. At every stop sellers would board the bus with baskets of bananas, peanuts, chargrilled corn and fried spicy snacks. Unperturbed by the over-crowding they inched their way over any obstacle and everyone shuffled round to accommodate them. Never once did I witness an angry look or any of the huffing and puffing that you come across on the London to Manchester.

I was at first curious, then sleepy, then fretful, then comatose, then tetchy and finally resigned. I was even beginning to enjoy the techno Hindi tracks that blared out from the radio. Tim made friends with the conductor who made sure that when the seat beside him became free it was occupied by a savoury character. Amin, the conductor, lives on the bus. Seven days a week he travels the route, sleeping on the back seats at each destination every night. He has no home but is glad of the job; he has a modicum of responsibility and he does it well. He told us he was poor because he was honest.

His English was unfortunately very good. I say unfortunately because he regaled us for an hour with stories of collisions and mass destruction on the Nepalese highways. We still had seven more hours to go and I really didn't want to know this. Two days before, a bus jumped (his words) over a bridge railing, falling into the river and killing five people. We saw buses that had collided with other buses, buses that had toppled over in a ditch and, the most distressing sight of all, a bicycle completely flattened lying at the side of the road. That shut us up for a bit and I vowed to be stricter with my helmet wearing.

Every few hours we were allowed to disembark for a pee stop; this was fine for Tim and Lee who joined the line of men at the side of the road. It was also fine for the ladies who only had to hoik up their saris and squat down on their haunches but I was in trousers. I became the mistress of resourcefulness; any bush no matter how low lying, someone's garden, a derelict shack, anywhere, just to get away from fascinated eyes. We eventually arrived and the bicycles were placed back on terra firma but, like a face where every wrinkle tells a story, the bikes were now a trilogy of scratches.

There was one issue which was beginning to worry me; I had not gone to the loo for ten days. It was getting uncomfortable, my belly was distended beyond all proportion and I felt irritable and cheated. I could hear the boys going four times a day. They came out of the bathroom looking pale and shaky but I could tell they were titillated by what they had delivered. It was all wrong. Who comes to this part of the world and gets constipation? I had to ban them from talking about their achievements as I lay in bed gripped by colonic spasms.

The next day we were to leave the haven of Nepal and cross the border into India. I had the feeling that it was time to face my fears and to see what I was made of. Nepal was a rehearsal for tougher things to come. We had met people along the way who described Nepal as a breeze compared to India, and I could well believe them. I have always been afraid of India, afraid of the poverty and human atrocities, certain that I would recoil from the challenge and spend every minute wishing I were somewhere else. If I only knew what lay in store I would have got on the next plane home.

'The sole country under the sun that is endowed with imperishable interest for alien prince and alien peasant, for lettered and ignorant, wise and fool, rich and poor, bond and free, the one land all men desire to see, and having seen once, by even a glimpse, would not give that glimpse for the shows of all the rest of the globe combined.'

Mark Twain

1897

5
DARJEELING, THE QUEEN OF THE HILLS

At dawn we cycled up to the bridge and silhouetted figures appeared out of the swirling mists. The span was not far but India remained invisible. The customs office was a small hut, we filled in our details; we were the fifth group of foreigners of the year to cross at that point.

Once over the bridge we had arrived in West Bengal and the change was immediate. There seemed to be more order, people owned their animals and there were more private cars on the road. On either side lay lush tea plantations, a table-flat carpet of dense, level bushes. The atmosphere felt more industrious, the people had tasks to achieve that day instead of marking time; I felt more akin to them.

Our destination that day was the hill station of Darjeeling, a climb of 2,300 metres, the highest I would ever be by bike. We started the climb at midday, it was baking hot.

Darjeeling perches on top of the 'Queen of Hills' - another fitting name. The hill is certainly regal and, if one can put a gender to it, definitely a woman. The climb was subtle and the road enticing, luring us around every bend like a sexy swagger from undulating hips. We rode past pastel wooden houses, glaring white Buddhist stupas, Hindi shrines and schools, following the toy train track that switch-backed up the mountainside. This was the other way to reach Darjeeling but there was a shortage of coal so the train only ran intermittently. The journey takes eight hours to go eighty kilometres, sometimes going so slowly that hawkers sell their goods alongside.

Like a woman the road cautioned; every few kilometres we came across yellow-painted signs embedded in the mountainside: 'Do not sleep. Your family will weep' and other such homilies, 'Hurry burry spoils the curry' and never a truer word than 'Keep your nerve on a sharp curve.'

On the day we rode up to Darjeeling was a special festival in honour of Saraswati - the goddess of literature, poetry, song and music. She is always to be seen smiling happily, a book and writing paper in one hand, a stringed instrument in the other. She sits on a swan symbolising that she is in control of her passions; the Hindus believe this to be a rightful condition for the success of any artistic endeavour. Hmm – I made a mental note to tell that to the next feverish choreographer who rants and raves all day long in a studio. Saraswati is also associated with the Peacock, the Indian royal bird admired for its unsurpassed beauty. Her swan floats on clear, still waters signifying lucidity of mind and clarity of expression. And so what god could possibly be man enough to stand by her side? Brahma, of course, the creator and the most revered of all gods. No wonder Saraswati is celebrated by young girls, the woman has it all.

Indian pop music mixed in with techno Hindi blared out across the mountainside and there were throngs of people dancing along the way. The sound quality was not high on the list of priorities; the hideous distortion didn't seem to bother them at all so long as it was loud. Makeshift shrines had been lovingly and imaginatively constructed like stalls at a village fete. Curiously the goddess Saraswati was often adorned with *Titanic* memorabilia, the connection of which was lost on me; I was just thankful that, although her swan had three large funnels poking out from behind, we were saved from pictures of Leo and Kate[1].

The road was often perilous. Every few kilometres we came across major roadworks and our skinny tyres skidded on the loose chippings that flew off and dropped down to the valley far below.

After a few hours of climbing my stomach cramps from being constipated were becoming unbearable; I felt quite faint with the pain

[1] Leonardo De Caprio and Kate Winslet – stars of the film *Titanic*

and had to stop every few kilometres to whinge. It did not help my psychological state that the gap between the boys and me was growing beyond all resurrection. At every tea stop I would set off at least ten minutes before them but all too soon I would look over my shoulder and see their hunched forms catching up until they inevitably overtook me. I had begun to memorise every vertebra of Tim's back, I watched the tendons in his hips become more pronounced and his calf muscles reshape so that they resembled a country bread roll, the ones that have a deep crevice down the middle. If this bodily transformation was happening to him then surely it was having the same effect on me. Uh oh! Was I developing cycler's thighs? I was worried I was going to start a fixation.

A friend of mine, also a dancer, took a year out from doing musicals to travel Australia in a combie van. She was one of those dancers paranoid about putting on weight but she didn't want her boyfriend to know it. Obviously travelling with a set of scales in the back of the van was out of the question so instead she took with her an old black skirt that fitted her exactly around the waist. Every few days she would sneak round the back of the combie and whip on her skirt to use it as her fatness gauge. If it became tight she knew to decline the extra steak on the barbie and fit in ten zillion more sit-ups during the day. I knew that I couldn't scale mountains without inviting some muscular abnormalities; I just fervently hoped that mine were on the imperceptible side.

I do not know whether it is a dancing mechanism but on every hill and every incline I found myself counting to a rhythm: a waltz perhaps or sometimes a march, 'Pedal...two, three. Pedal...two, three.' In dancing, to take our minds away from shaky legs and bursting lungs, we latch onto the rhythm of the music to carry us through to the end. With athletes perhaps it is the rhythm of winning that they run with.

But now that I was cycling it was beginning to drive me crazy; this was the time to let my mind roam free. But I found that I couldn't, no matter how hard I tried my mind kept returning to counting. My internal conversations went something like this:

'That poor dog has had so many litters that her teats are practically dragging along the ground...one, two...one, two. I wonder if we're nearly at the top....Pedal...two, three, four. Pedal...six, seven, eight. AARRGGHH!'

I ground to a halt, now completely doubled-over in cramps. Tim had slowed down in anxious sympathy. I was indulging in a sorry-for-myself weep when a young boy interrupted me and looked earnestly into my face. I went to move on but he stopped me and offered a newspaper cone filled with sugared wheat. Now that contact had been initiated his sister boldly came over and anointed my forehead with crusty, henna dye. I smiled waterily and struggled on my way.

Everywhere was shut because of the holiday but we eventually caught up with Lee who had managed to secure us an omelette from a local shopkeeper. We clambered up a ladder to a tiny room at the back of the shack and found sweet tea, omelettes and stale white bread waiting for us. Our gracious hosts stared in disbelief as we wolfed down the food. I'm afraid we were not very good ambassadors for Britain; dirty, tear-stained cheeks, smudged Hindi spot, various layers of cycling gear and voracious appetites. The grandmother seemed the most perplexed, she was used to the British officers and their genteel wives coming up to the sanatorium of Darjeeling to escape the heat and the dust of the northern plains.

There was no way we were going to reach Darjeeling that day so we found a hotel half way up. I could now hardly stand up straight and sent the boys off to find laxatives, if such a medicine exists in India. Meanwhile I drank pots of coffee and contorted myself into Yogic twists in an attempt to excite my colon into action. Nothing happened.

That night over dinner just as we were about to tuck into our first meal on Indian ground I spotted a rat scuttle along the skirting board in hot pursuit of a cockroach. I suddenly lost my appetite and began to scrutinise every piece of cutlery and crockery on the table. Huge mistake. What the eye doesn't see the mind doesn't know. I felt the beginnings of a cleanliness obsession rising in me as I picked over my food, only eating what had not come into contact with the plate. This was something that I knew I would have to overcome if I wanted to keep my strength up.

The next morning we set off early to finish the climb. I relished every part of it, it was a road of utter uniqueness; breathtaking views down to the plains, friendly faces at every corner. At one point I went into over-drive (or over-cycle), as six young boys ran behind me pushing me faster. I shot past Tim and Lee, smiling gaily and accompanied with squeals of delight from the boys. To the left was a sea of tea estates, to the right the adolescent ridge of the mountains that then matured into the Himalayas. We now drank Darjeeling tea, a subtle perfumed brew.

Tea came to this part of the world in a fantastical way. A Brahmin went as a missionary to China but before reaching his destination he was so tired that he fell asleep. When he awoke he was so angry with himself for dallying that he tore out his own eyebrows in a fit of self-loathing. The eyebrows took root and grew into tea plants. The Brahmin, once his anger had subsided, was so hungry that he ate the leaves. He immediately fell into meditation whilst tea bushes shot up around him.

Just before reaching Darjeeling we stopped to eat a mid-morning snack at the town of Ghoom. The pageant of Saraswati had caught up with us so I danced in the street with the kids hoping that I would become more beautiful, my creative passion more harnessed and the god of all gods might materialise before me and put a wedding ring on my finger. Instead my saddle sores burst into fire and I bickered with Tim for shooting off too fast.

'Where do you live?'

'I live in Darjeeling.'

Can you imagine saying that or writing it at the bottom of your address? To me Darjeeling was another of those places with an impossibly pretty name that seemed to conjure up all manner of exotic secrets. I wondered if it was the tea connection but Orange Pekoe didn't trigger off the same sparks of excitement. No, it was definitely the placing of the right consonants next to the right amount of vowels, the same as Kathmandu, which made me want to say it over and over again.

But in case I got bored of saying Darjeeling then I could call it by its other name 'Place of the Thunder Bolt.' Not such a pretty name but ten out of ten for the element of drama. I tried to think of an alias for Chiswick: 'Place of the Constant Drizzle with the Odd Bout of Sunshine' or perhaps, 'Place of the Never-ending Row of Overpriced Restaurants.'

Darjeeling straddles a ridge of the Himalayas and has been a summer hill station since 1837. The British declared it their haven and set about making it a home away from home. It was the perfect place to come for rest and relaxation. They did a good job. I felt like I had entered an exotic, mountainous Cheltenham. Gracious Victorian buildings lined the cobbled streets interrupted by Buddhist Gompas on whose balconies young monks leaned over, waving at us. Everywhere you looked there were narrow flights of steps leading this way and that, old British Land Rovers flew down narrow streets making pedestrians leap backwards disturbing the monkeys as they enjoyed a quiet munch on an orange.

At the top of the town was the Chowrasta – a small square surrounded by elegant shops, pony and traps and Victorian street lamps. This was where crown princes promenaded fresh-faced young English girls. This was where the jubilee celebrations took place for King George V. The diversity of this magical place delighted every part of me. I could relive the nostalgic glamour of this far-flung outpost of the British Empire or I could go in search of the other side to Darjeeling, the Darjeeling which is the home to many Nepalese, the Darjeeling which provides a new home for many Tibetans who fled here in the wake of the Chinese invasion and the home to many of the Gurkhas who thrive on the high altitude and mountain air. On every spare bit of mountainside stood a monastery. This Himalayan ridge was deemed the ideal spot; nearer to the heavens to get closer to purity and far away from the licentious temptations of the northern plains.

In the evening, as we stood at the top of a flight of steps dressed in every item of clothing in our panniers to keep out the bitter night air, we stopped to listen to the strains of chanting floating out across the ridge, one monastery echoing the other. I felt like I was on a film set waiting for the director's orders over the mega-phone, 'OK let's call it a wrap' and then to watch the flat-faced Tibetans whip off their balaclavas and blankets and shout out to each other across the square, 'Oi! Tony, fancy a beer and a game of pool?' But instead the air resonated with an empathy for all the different stories that had been lived out on this remote spot, the hearts that had been broken, the solace that had been found, the happiness regained and the sanity restored.

Tim had not been feeling so good since we arrived; he had spent the day dragging his feet along in an exhausted fever. Lee had suffered the same symptoms a few days before and, although we came to the conclusion that it was nothing serious, they both felt pretty wretched and depleted. Tim went to bed shivering under layers of Gurkha regiment blankets, silent and withdrawn.

This provided the first opportunity to spend some time alone and I felt my mind drifting to the situation we were in. This was a strange time for Tim and me without doubt; he was returning home after a four-year absence. He had made a name for himself in London, he was the new hotshot Head Chef in one of the best vegetarian restaurants in the country. He loved his work, he had great friends and he had grown to love the city. And now he had to give it all up to return home to obscurity once again. He was leaving me behind as well, not sure as to whether I would follow him or not.

I had put it into my head that this trip would be a test of our relationship; I wanted it to certify one hundred percent that we were a great couple and that, geography aside, we were meant to be together. And yet there were so many more pressing things to contend with that the main reason for embarking on this trip occupied the smallest of spaces in my mind. I was feeling the pace a challenge but I was adamant that Tim and Lee would not feel the need to pander to my female sensibilities. It took all of my strength to keep up and to keep quiet. I preferred to lapse into long silences and daydreams rather than make conversation which was unusual for me who normally feels the need to fill any silence. I asked Tim if he had noticed. He had of course, wondering what was going through my mind. There seemed to be no energy left over to love or to be loved.

That night, as I sat at one of the mahogany bridge tables in the colonial drawing room of the Hotel Windermere with Tim tucked up in bed in a cheaper version further up the town, I tried to sum up how good a time we were having together. I wanted every minute to be fantastic and romantic and wonderful so I would not be beset with indecision once we were parted. I knew the reality of having such high ideals was ridiculous but I couldn't help but be aware of my doubts: the age difference was too big, the way he ate too noisy, his walk too ungainly. These were neurotic, inconsequential things and I knew he would have a similar set for me. But was it possible not to have any doubts at all?

One of the things to do in Darjeeling is to get up just before dawn and catch a jeep up to Tiger Hill to watch the sun rise over Kanchenjunga, the third highest mountain in the world. Not wanting a repetition of the Annapurnas we set our alarm at 4.15 am and along with two podgy Indian tourists we caught a jeep to take us up there. Sadly it was not the earth moving experience I had anticipated. By the time we had arrived Tiger Hill was a writhing mass of middle class Indians on holiday all supping tea out of white plastic cups that when discarded, in the dawn light, looked like a blanket of snow. Everyone stood around with an air of expectancy, shivering in the freezing morning air. Unfortunately we had picked the mistiest morning to view one of the first places on the earth to reflect the sun. However at about 6.30 am the first peaks of the Himalayan range loomed out of the cauldron of mist. As the sun rose the peak of Kanchenjunga appeared to a round of applause. It didn't look attached to this earth but lowered from the sky, suspended in mid-air.

I was doing a spot of people watching when a young Indian gentleman tapped me on the shoulder.

'Please sister, may I have picture please with you sister?'

I accepted, I hope graciously, although I hadn't reckoned on being surrounded by twenty other young men who had appeared from nowhere. I gestured towards Tim and Lee suggesting to the photographer and his mates that they be included as well. This was obviously not what they had in mind as they squeezed and inched their way around me managing to completely block Tim and Lee from the frame. I wondered if perhaps this photo would be handed out around a computer course classroom and myself proclaimed as some sort of love trophy.

Later in the day Tim and I went to do some shopping. We had both fallen in love with Buddhist *thangkas*, *thang* being the Tibetan word for sacred writing and *ka* meaning record. They are intricate paintings set in a wall-hanging of silk and are regarded as the essence of reverence, a medium through which the highest ideals of Buddhism are evoked. It takes a monk one year to complete a *thangka*. First the canvas is prepared by boiling it with rice water then beating it against a rock; this process is repeated daily for one month. Quartz stone and other materials are then pulverised before the actual painting of tiny Buddhas, the tips of the Himalayas, the temples and the lotus leaves can be started.

A *thangka* is a powerful meditation device, a visual aid to hone the concentration to introvertive questioning thus leading to a greater understanding of the self and the supernatural forces. They adorn the walls of every temple, the silk surround impregnated with years of burning incense. They also hang in the homes of the ordinary folk who believe they bring peace and protection and as a reminder that Nirvana can only be found by their own efforts. Sometimes the shopkeeper goes personally to Tibet to bring them back, other times the lamas bring them over themselves, enduring a nine-day walk and a long journey by yak. One lama did the journey only to reach the border where a Chinese official tore it in two. One year's work ruined.

By this time their obvious beauty had magnified in our eyes and we had set our hearts on owning one. But then came the big dilemma - to buy one together or to buy one each? We both became very quiet, avoiding each other's eyes and pouring our concentration into picking up other objects in the shop, meanwhile our minds were working furiously. I knew that if the object in question were a wok, a bed or a computer then automatically we would have paid half each. But this *thangka* was so much more than a utensil, we wanted one in our lives but were we prepared to take the chance of something going wrong between us? As it turned out - No! An innocent shopping spree had suddenly turned into a question of commitment.

I thought that by buying something of such personal importance together signified the end of an era of my life, the end of Polly Benge who I had lived with for twenty-nine years. I know that there must come a time when you relinquish your sense of self, a sense of self only in the egotistical way, the 'this is mine and I do this, and these are my friends' sort of way. But to me it signified an important watershed. And so we went for the soft option; we bought one each. They were both slightly different; our *thangkas* would stand up easily on their own but would compliment each other perfectly if placed side by side. Perhaps a good relationship is as simple as that, and maybe, inadvertently, Tim and I had just taken a large step forward in the lessons of love.

The food in Darjeeling was delicious. It was a touristy area so I felt I could take off my Hygiene Inspector hat for a while. In between our constant tea drinking we ate subtle and delicate Tibetan soups, scalding hot *samosas* and *pokoras* cooked on the roadside, and vast Indian *thalis*, each dish housing spicy and aromatic curries. Our greed got the better of us when we came across a distant cousin of 'Ye Olde Tea Shoppe' and bought a box of doughnuts. I suppose it was only fitting that I got the non-vegetarian option, I counted fifteen ants in my jam. But I was getting hardier; I fished them out and then continued to enjoy what was left.

Gentle Darjeeling, I was sad to say goodbye. As we flew down the hill, *thangkas* strapped to the back of our bikes, I found it hard to imagine that at the bottom of this Queen of Hills thousands of civil servants, millions of 'Untouchables,' ascetics and soldiers wept and slept, hungered and died, dated and procreated on a scale only the sub-continent could carry. The road that took us nearly two days to climb disappeared under our wheels in four hours.

"Behind the blinds I sit and watch

The people passing – passing by;

And not a single one can see

My tiny watching eye."

Walter De La Mere
'The Window', 1913

6
INTO THE BELLY OF INDIA

Hell's kitchen is the only way to describe Siliguri. It was dusk and rush hour. The air became dusty, a pollution soup that stung our eyes and clogged our throats. The roads were ordered chaos, split into nine lanes structured on a strict caste basis. In descending order: pedestrians, legless bodies strapped to wheeled trolleys, cart pushers, bicycles that carried things like bamboo poles or three-piece suites, rickshaws, single bicycles, mopeds, cars, then buses and trucks. We switched on our dynamo lights and launched ourselves in.

After the initial terror wore off I quite enjoyed the sensation of absolute concentration. Every nerve-ending was on alert, my mind only full of the task at hand, my eyes like flies and stomach contracted. I felt razor sharp. Lee was ahead, Tim behind and the entire cast of Wacky Racers on either side. In the gathering darkness our fellow commuters could not figure out what we were; we had lights but no motor, we were going as fast as the cars but had no horn. 'What is this type of transporting please sir?' There were no traffic regulations - only to keep on going, feeding in when necessary. God help whoever upsets the flow. This river knew only one speed, go against it and it would spit you out.

The atmosphere was like an antiquated sci-fi movie; the buildings were all on one level, low, and built from wood. There were food stalls and shacks lit by paraffin lanterns, people huddled around fires and we passed an empty rickshaw stadium like a deserted Park and Ride on the outskirts of Oxford. The Creator had put a red light bulb in the sky that night.

We found a shabby hotel and Tim collapsed. I felt duty bound to persuade him to lay off the *lassis*, he had become a dedicated *lassi* lover, but I feared that they were the cause of his demise. Lee and I ate spicy noodles sitting on the curb, watching mangy dogs and even mangier kids. The little girls' dresses must once have been spectacular; it seemed to be a common trend to see how many frills one can put on a frock.

The next day we were heading out to Assam. It was time to tackle the most famous conveyor belt in the world, the Indian railways. This vast, state-run conglomerate is the largest single employer in the world and moves ten million people a day. British colonialists laid most of the 62,000 kilometres of track leaving a legacy of sturdy Victorian relics: large station clocks, scales and benches.

We knew there was some complicated system attached to buying a ticket but for the life of us we could not work it out. A fellow traveller gave us some handy advice.

'You don't need First Class AC in the winter, I recommend Second Class Two Tier and I wouldn't go Second Class AC Three Tier if I were you. But whatever you do, don't go Third Class Unreserved.'

We went Third Class Unreserved, not by design, nor for any altruistic reasons to gaze and marvel at the cruel, human element of India, but because of our ineptitude at deciphering the bureaucracy and because we met Pinkie. Wonderful, kind, maddening Pinkie.

As Tim fended off the hundreds of curious hands mauling our bikes outside the station, Lee and I went to get the tickets. Lee was convinced that one of my talents would be confident queue manoeuvring. Not wanting to go down in his expectations I eventually managed to push my way to the kiosk. As I waved a fistful of rupees through the bars a Chinese looking woman took us by the hand and declared herself our guide.

'I know this, I help you. You my brothers and sister - who knows I may die tomorrow!'

Pinkie (we never did find out her real name) was a Tibetan Buddhist living in Shillong, the capital city of Meghalaya. She was a bright and vivacious woman prone to shrieks of laughter at the slightest provocation; her sole aim in life was getting a plane ticket to America or Britain, convinced that wealth and happiness is dished out over every counter. The fact that we were travelling on the same train was the next best thing; she had her very own 'westies' for the day and she was not going to let us out of her sight. She had a clothes shop in Shillong, selling western clothes of course, and commuted to Kathmandu via Siliguri for regular buying sprees. Confused and rather fazed we fell into her capable hands.

The system dictated that we send our bicycles on the train ahead. Why? I have absolutely no idea. In the post room multitudes of forms were filled in, stickers stuck on every available part, labels tied onto handlebars, 'Old, Used and Unpacked.' At this, Lee visibly baulked; his made to measure bike cost him £1,000 and more. How could this work of art be relegated to such a lowly description? We were asked the monetary value of our bicycles but we were too embarrassed to tell them the real amount. As it was we halved the amount but still the officers were flabbergasted.

'I am thinking these bicycles are very, very costly sir.'

Our train was only two hours late, a mere wisp of time compared to the twenty-two hour delay of the day before. It gave us a chance to enjoy the platform spectacle. The first sensory onslaught was the smell, a pot-pourri of urine and faeces that emanated from the smouldering heaps on the tracks. When the trains left the station a quiet, industrious peace settled over the platform. Small clusters of men squatted in front of chairs, their makeshift kitchens, to spoon freshly cooked *chana* into plastic bags, the Indian snack equivalent to a bag of chips. Another group were brewing tea, others furiously making *chapatis*. Once a train pulled in furore broke out. The passengers spilt out onto the platform rushing to the row of taps to wash their faces before having a cup of tea and a snack. Fathers held their little boys to piss against the side of the train. The peddlers broke into their selling mantras: '*Chana, chana, chana, chana.*', '*Roti, roti, roti, roti.*'

We gingerly boarded the train, gagging at the urine smell impregnated into the small confines of the carriage. Pinkie hustled us into some seats, looking proud of herself and superior next to her fellow passengers, basking in the wake of her auspicious charges. We sat down on blue plastic benches and peered out through the iron bars covering the windows, there was no glass. Everywhere I looked there were dark faces peering at us; a fat woman lying in a bundle of sari on the top bunk, two beggar ragamuffins waiting for left over titbits at our feet, a couple of soldiers with pongy feet.

No matter what the nationality, what the religion, class, caste or otherwise, long train journeys unite. You share your boredom, your supply of food, your jokes and life ambitions with people you would not normally have the occasion to talk to. Indian trains are no exception. We were on this train for twelve hours and we got to know our travelling companions pretty well. The man opposite me was a charity worker and member of Amnesty International, a serious man who devoured my book whenever I wasn't reading it. We offered him Horlicks biscuits, he offered us cigarettes; we felt bad that none of us smoked. Next to him sat a very proper gentleman with coarse salt-and-pepper hair and a bushy moustache; he worked in the Indian Air Force. At such close quarters it was hard not to stare as he surreptitiously removed his false teeth to eat some home-made cake.

It soon became evident that Pinkie was a man-eater; she was holding court, fluttering her eyelashes at the soldiers and playfully slapping the pilot. But the object of her desires was Lee. To him all attention was bestowed, to him were her songs directed, for him did she buy the sticky *ras gulla* sweets. She was rather hazy about her relationship status; we could definitely make out that she had two children and we were led to believe she had a husband but, 'I have so many boyfriends sister.' she said to me in a conspiratorial manner.

'Look this ring, so beautiful. This ring given to me by one of my so many boyfriends. I have such lovely boyfriend called Peter. Maybe you know him, he lives in Australia?'

'Oh, Australia is not in England?'

Unperturbed she launched into a song, "Dancing Queen, young and lean, only seventeen." Hey brother, (addressed to Lee) you know this Abba song? Which girl you like best?'

There was no doubt about it Pinkie was a trip!

The soldiers with the smelly feet painted a different picture of love and marriage, more a financial union than anything else. One was married, happily or not was anyone's guess. His wife was picked for him when she was fourteen, the families were from the same caste and her dowry was attractive. His status as a soldier and university graduate meant that he could command a sizeable dowry. He told us about his cousin who was training to be a doctor. When it was time for him to marry he could bargain a medical degree and a Green Card, and then the dollar signs would start flashing big time. Both soldiers shook their heads at the very thought.

The other soldier was still single; he was in love with a girl who came from a poorer background. He feared that amassing her dowry would financially cripple her parents who would probably have to resort to the corrupt hands of the moneylenders. Death is not uncommon in this business of marriage. Fathers top themselves when the pressure gets too much; young girls kill themselves rather than send the family to rack and ruin. More horrific still is the practice of 'bride burning'.

Newspaper reports abound on women burning to death in their kitchens, allegedly from spilt kerosene. These crimes are often set up by greedy in-laws who want their sons to benefit from another dowry or another woman with more prospects and more boys in her womb. Other times it is suicide; the girls cannot bear to put up with any more undisguised disapproval from their in-laws, so death is preferable. The tradition of dowries is now illegal but they still remain an inherent part of Indian culture continuing to keep marriage a dark and gloomy affair.

The Hindu caste system is a complicated and mysterious concept for westerners to grasp. It is easy to jump to assumptions; the man sweeping the corridors of the train is of a lower caste than the plump tea-estate manager sitting a couple of carriages down. This is not always the case; a high caste Brahmin could be seen walking the streets half clothed whilst a Dalit or 'untouchable' could become president of a major company. The *Rig Veda*, the earliest book of the four *Vedas* (books of knowledge) records how the Brahmins or priest caste divided up the original single caste into four stages thus retaining their superiority in a society of declining morals.

The most superior and sophisticated are the Brahmins who decree what is right and wrong in matters of religion and caste. Then come the Kshatriyas who are the warrior caste, namely the soldiers and the administrators. Next are the Vaisyas who comprise skilled craftsmen and merchants and then the Sudras who are the peasants and the farmers.

In Hindu mythology each caste was born from the body of Brahma, the creator. Brahma resides in the underbelly of the sea. When he 'breathes out' the universe comes to life. He stays awake for one day, the equivalent of two billion human years, then 'breathes in' and gradually falls asleep again. He must have a busy day when he does wake; he manages to find time to be a husband to the beautiful Saraswati, he causes all that is in the world to exist as well as giving birth to the four different castes. From his mouth come the Brahmins, from his arms the Kshatriyas, from his thighs the Vaisyas and from his feet the Sudras.

Below the Sudras come the untouchables who belong to no caste, they carry out the most menial jobs and the tasks deemed as impure, such as dealing with dead animals or excrement. At the height of caste discrimination, if one was touched by an untouchable or even if their shadow crossed your path, you were considered polluted and had to be ritually cleansed. A verse in the *Upanishads* (ancient text from a book of the *Vedas*) stresses the contempt with which they were held.

"Those whose conduct on earth has given pleasure can hope to enter a pleasant womb, that is the womb of a Brahmin, or a woman of the princely caste.
But those whose conduct on earth has been foul can expect to enter a foul and stinking womb, that is, the womb of a bitch, or a pig, or an outcaste."

Gandhi came to their rescue and set about a mission to bring them into society. He renamed them Harijans or "Children of God". Gradually, as the demise of the caste system grew, the prospects of the Harijans improved. In the 1950 Indian Constitution untouchability was abolished and any discrimination punished. University places were now reserved for a large number of them, they were assigned jobs in national industries and they were entrusted with more responsibilities. They are now called 'Dalits' meaning 'oppressed' and their fate is regarded as important. However, in the backwaters of India the caste system still lives on and violent outbreaks continue to occur.

We were feeling very altogethery in our carriage so that when the blind piper came to play us some tunes we fell silent and gave him our full attention. The young man's eyes were covered in cataracts. The folk songs he played were pure and beautiful. I had to turn my face to look out at the passing Indian plains; I didn't want the others to see the tears streaming down my cheeks. I was crying for the poignancy of the music, the elixir of life and the perfection of that instant.

I climbed up to the bunk where Tim was sleeping and inched myself beside him. It was dusk outside and fat, juicy mosquitoes flew in through the window. I spent the last couple of hours drifting between sleep and consciousness, tears intermittently seeping and my heart full to bursting. A happiness so complete had sneaked up behind me and come to rest gently on my shoulder.

We arrived in Guwahati, the capital of Assam, from now on referred to as Sewerhati, close to midnight and my spell of universal love came to an abrupt end. The platform had doubled up as a dormitory and we had to pick our way over recumbent figures whilst shooing away the mosquitoes. With Pinkie still as our self-appointed squadron leader we set off to find our bicycles. From platform to platform, from store depot to left luggage, we traipsed; we received blank looks each time. I was consumed with the desire to be somewhere clean and gorgeous. My flirt with degradation did not want to flower into the full monty. I empathised with Robert Lutyens who came to India in 1937 to show the Maharaja of Jaipur his designs for a palace. In a letter he sent to his mother, the day after his arrival in India, he wrote:

"Now that I have seen India, can't I come home again?"

We did locate our bikes that night, and they looked old, used and unpacked. But amongst all the madness they presented a comforting sight, an emblem of stability in our ever-changing world.

Whilst pondering how best to ascend the stairs with bikes and luggage an old man, no taller than my shoulders, materialised in front of me. He gestured towards my bike, tapped his turban and without losing eye contact bowed his head. I have not witnessed such a theatrical

73

and camp performance since the Northern Ballet Theatre. I shook my head. He paused for an instant, gestured towards my bike, tapped his turban and without losing eye contact, bowed his head.

'No, no sir, it is much too heavy,' I didn't want to be responsible for his hernias.

Once again, the three precise movements and with each repetition the definition of his mouth became more stubborn. Oh well, if he did insist. I watched through slatted fingers as his spindly frame hoisted my laden bicycle on to the top of his head. With a waver and a stumble he righted himself. We were all on the alert, ready to jump in with our ABC of First Aid: check his airways, look for broken bones and then offer him a *chapati*. He was my Hercules; he made it up the stairs then down the other side. His eyes perhaps bulged more, and his neck compacted a couple of centimetres, but he was triumphant.

Pinkie promised to take us to, 'very good hotel sister.' On the way I spotted a rat the size of a dachshund with a perpendicular tail picking its way through the gutters. It is the same wherever you are in the world; areas around a central station are notoriously seedy. We should have realised this as Pinkie led us through the fetid streets of Sewerhati. We were given the luxury room, the extra rupees ensuring a collection of fag ends on the table and empty liquor bottles on the floor. I spent half an hour sewing up the holes in my mosquito net and preferred to go to bed dirty rather than succumbing to the stinking hell-hole of the bathroom.

India does little for your sex life. There should be a warning below the 'multiple entry' section of your visa. I would salute any woman who could come to India and feel sexy. The filth and the squalor are not conducive to passionate tussling. Too much flailing of the limbs tears away the sheets leaving hot, sweaty bodies lying on grimy mattresses. I don't think men are put off by stained sheets or strip lights, but I was. My lack of libido was not just an aversion to dirt, I felt rather overwhelmed by the coupling of my surroundings with myself to then enter into erotic intimacy with another human being.

And yet India hums with the whispers of sensuality; one just has to look at the temples decorated with the acts of lovemaking and the erotic monuments displaying gargantuan phalluses. Beneath these gasp-inducing displays of sexuality lie stories of trembling bodies made suppliant under the fervent hands of love gods. Passionate love songs used to be read out every evening at dusk on the temple steps so that all castes could be consumed by Bhakti, the ecstatic love of God. And then there is the erotic poem of Gita Govinda, the story of Krishna's early life as a cowherd and the infatuation of a milkmaid called Radha. Radha's longing for Govinda's perfect body possessed her until every waking moment was consumed with the thought of him. Unfortunately his passion for milkmaids did not stop with her. She would wait and wait for him, imploring her friends to make him come to her. Sometimes she would wait in vain, other times he would come still with the vestiges of other milkmaids' pleasure on his body.

It was easy to become intoxicated, to bask in a sensuality that was so much more subtle than the consumer excesses of home; expressive hands, vermilion cloth, dark shapely midriffs, attar of sandalwood, the rustle of bamboo and the smell of evening.

Tim found a poem:

"Her breath is like honey spiced with cloves.
Her mouth delicious as a ripened mango
To press kisses on her skin is to taste the lotus
The deep cave of her navel hides a store of spices
What pleasure lies beyond, the tongue knows
But cannot speak of."

Srngarakarika Kumaradadatta 12th Century

I wanted to succumb, to languish with Tim in this sensual headiness, if only to feed off these memories and to keep my fire burning once we were parted.

"It is difficult to believe in the dreadful but quiet war of organic beings, going on in the peaceful woods, and smiling fields."

Darwin
Journal entry, 1839

7

MR AND MRS PINKIE

Here we were in northeast India, the most unstable region in the whole of the subcontinent. It lies at the feet of the Himalayas. It brushes shoulders with Burma and walks side by side with Bangladesh. Through the centre runs the mighty Brahmaputra, one of the widest rivers in the world, its many tributaries running out like spilt ink on a blotter. The biggest state is Assam, 'Land of the Red River and the Blue Hills'; it is home to some of the most violent uprisings in modern day India.

From the earliest of times Assam has been a melting pot of different races. It has endured a host of invasions by the Burmese, the Mongoloids, the Ahoms from northern Thailand and the British. During the Anglo-Burmese war of 1824 Burma handed over a large section of northeast India to the British including Assam. In World War II it played an important part as a supply route to Burma and China.

The British realised that they had inherited a region abundant in natural resources. When an English officer was out on patrol one day he noticed a brown, sticky substance in the footprints of his elephant. He commanded his chowdikkar to investigate, 'Dig boy!' The boy dug and came across oil. The place was called Digboi and remains with that name to this day.

The rich soil was cultivated into three hundred tea plantations; hundreds of acres of malaria-infested swamp and tropical jungle were transformed into neat and ordered tea gardens. But in transforming this inhospitable terrain rifts in the state began to surface. The indigenous Assamese are a proud and self-sufficient lot; they refused to work in the tea plantations thinking the work too lowly for them, instead the jobs were given out to eager Bengalis and other thankful people from central India.

Then in 1905 the British Governor of Bengal partitioned Bengal and attached several of its eastern districts to Assam. A new province was created – Assam and East Bengal. This partitioning was not popular on both sides and invited violent protests. In 1911 the partitioning was reversed and all of the rightful states handed back to Bengal. But over the years Bengalis started pouring back into Assam of their own accord, seeking settlement in the relatively sparsely populated area. Add to these, Bangladeshi immigrants who fled into Assam to escape the poverty of their own country after Indira Gandhi opened the borders in 1979. They wanted land of their own, they wanted the right to vote and of course, they wanted jobs. The census showed that Assam's population was rapidly growing at a rate much higher than that of the rest of India. The ethnic Assamese, especially the students, were clearly alarmed and anti-immigration agitation flared up. Billboards with the slogan "Jobs for the Boys" were put up all over the state. They feared they were in danger of becoming a minority.

For the last thirty years Assam has been subjected to severe violence. The United Liberation Front of Assam – plus other groups – have organised a number of militant operations around the state, fighting for independence. They kept the Indian army on the run for many years but the government mounted a series of raids to flush out the guerrillas. The ULFA was suppressed for a while but only to regroup some years later to carry out more bombings and kidnappings.

Meanwhile trouble was simmering from a different part of the state; Assamese nationalism sparked off undisguised animosity from the tribals, mainly the Bodos. These hillsmen felt that they had been callously neglected by the state of Assam itself. It was as if they had suddenly woken up and realised they had missed the boat; the wealthy tea-estate owners and export merchants were reaping the benefits of their rightful land. The tribe's people fought for autonomy, statehood and independence. The Nagars struggled for complete independence and won; they now have a separate state called Nagarland. The Bodo's are still fighting for Bodoland but the government is not relenting. They continue to fight their cause in a bloody and terror-invoking fashion. Assam was declared a no-go area.

No one, it seems, is safe from the impassioned hands of the Bodos. They strike at any time of day or night, stealing into unsuspecting tea gardens and shooting the owners in cold blood. They blow up bridges on major highways and kidnap anyone with money or power.

We knew the history, we knew of the political situation, yet still we went. Ignorance is the mother of all adventure. We had one tip-off from a man back home, Finn, who from his experience two years ago told us the situation was fine. What we didn't know was that his definition of fine was far removed from ours, or that he thrived on adrenaline inducing skirmishes.

A couple of weeks before we left we met him in a pub off the Harrow Road so that he could give us his notes of the route. We sat and listened to his stories; he talked of quiet roads of breathtaking beauty, he talked of drinking tea with pygmy tribals, of rafting down fresh water rivers, elephant rides at dawn and unsurpassed cycling. He warned us of cerebral malaria, of nights spent huddled underneath mosquito nets, he warned us of taking the wrong road and ending up in the middle of the jungle but he did not warn us of serious danger. We had to find that out for ourselves.

Before cycling around Assam, we were going to cycle for ten days in a big loop around the state of Meghalaya. We had given ourselves exactly ten days to do the route as Lee's girlfriend Glenna was coming out to travel Assam with us. We had the envelope with Finn's notes inside and his words of warning ringing in our ears.

'Once you're on the route there is no turning back.'

We wondered what this meant.

Meghalaya means "Abode of the Clouds" and is the northeast's predominant tribal area. It was previously part of Assam but became a separate state in 1972. Meghalaya is inhabited by three tribal groups: the Garos in the west who are of Tibetan stock, (they are animists and once practiced human sacrifice), the Khasis in the centre who are related to the Shans of Burma and the Jaintias in the east. These tribes sought sanctuary in the hills and forests of Meghalaya, having migrated from their own countries hundreds of years of ago. They continue to live in their matriarchal society and live completely off the land, far, far removed from the rest of civilisation.

Like Assam, Meghalaya was also closed to tourists unless you were given a special permit from the government. The state was beset with terrorist and militant operations. The tribals of Meghalaya also wanted their own slice of the pie. Garo nationalists fighting for a separate state launch ambushes from the dense banana and bamboo jungle on an almost daily basis. As it is, in this already tiny state, three different languages are spoken in a radius of a hundred miles. The extremists are predominantly young men and one cannot help but question whether they are committed to their cause or just bored.

Because of its proximity to Assam, the Garo and Khasi hills provide ideal hiding places for the UFLA from the government as well as a good looting ground at night for passing trucks. Although the troubles in Meghalaya are much more under control we were told that it would be advisable to let some of the state dignitaries know of our route and also to get permission to stay in government run buildings. Where our route was taking us there were no hotels or even lodges. The place to get this permission is Shillong, the capital of Meghalaya and home of Pinkie. Very fortuitous.

'Please, I help you, you my brothers and sister. Who knows we may die tomorrow.'

All this talk of impending death was beginning to irk me, I hoped that she was not seeing something untoward with her third eye. She bundled us into a taxi for the four hour drive up through pineapple plantations to Shillong.

Shillong was another hill station in colonial times. Nicknamed 'Scotland of the East' for the abundance of pine trees and similarities to English weather. As each kilometre took us further away from Sewerhati, we found ourselves being able to breathe once more. Often when you put yourselves into the hands of someone else it can be a fine line between help and hindrance. Pinkie was so eager to please that a simple procedure took twice as long. We arrived in Shillong five minutes before the offices of the District Commissioner were due to shut. We were told, with no sense of irony that the officers come to work late and leave early, we had to come back tomorrow.

If you were to walk around Shillong you would notice that the women were clothed in a curious type of dress; a sort of hybrid blend of a Liberty print shirt-waister and a sari. We were told the story later that night. When the British first came across Shillong the natives went about largely naked. Wanting to clothe these savages before instructing them on how to create their golf courses, they dropped down pieces of cloth from their aeroplanes. The hill people, not knowing about clothes, draped the cloth around them tying a knot at each shoulder. Thus was born the Shillong style of dress that still remains unique to the area. In the winter months they put tartan shawls around their shoulders, another British legacy that is reluctant to die.

Pinkie insisted that we stayed the night with her and her family. Perhaps this would shed some light on her family affairs. I was very excited. She paraded us up her street, introducing us to the vegetable seller, the *paan* wallah, the school kids and anyone who looked remotely interested. Her house was a patchwork of clapboard, each wall painted a different colour and inside, posters of alpine purity were stuck up all over the place. Her children were seriously enchanting, bright as buttons and instilled with the Buddhist precepts. The Dalai Lama had blessed them (from what I could gather this took place over the phone) with his own name – Tenzing. There was the girl, Tenzing Balsam, and the boy, Tenzing Nola.

At home Pinkie's longing for westernism seemed to be more subdued. It was as if the very foundations of her house and the demands of her children were her anchor to this adopted world, already so much more western than her native Tibet. Later in the evening her husband came home, a terrifyingly gaunt figure with sunken cheeks, no teeth and a straggly ponytail hanging down his back. No wonder Pinkie had boyfriends. They did not embrace, they did not speak, no warmth or love emanated from either of them.

He stared at us for a long time, unnerving us with his silent presence. We covered our unease by lavishing attention on the Tenzings. Gradually he began to speak. In perfect English he talked of his beloved Tibet which he had to flee when he was seven, his longing to go home and to take his children with him. But he could not see it happening in his lifetime and also feared that the culture would be too different for them, the altitude too high and the geography too remote. He spoke of his worries once the Dalai Lama dies; he felt the government only tolerates the Tibetans because the spiritual leader of the world has chosen to live in India. But the Dalai Lama is old and when he dies how would the new one come to be recognised now that the Tibetans were scattered all over the sub-continent?

Dalai Lama means 'Great Ocean Superior One.' When Tibet was an independent state the Dalai Lama was its ruler. Chosen by the people of Tibet, the state investigators travelled to every village in the kingdom to find a child that was born at the exact time that the old Dalai Lama had passed away. He had to be born with certain features and characteristics in common with his predecessor; he also had to recognise some of the objects that the old Dalai Lama possessed. If he passed this complex set of qualifications then the Council would be assured that this was indeed the reincarnation of the great leader, the old 'spirit' had died but returned to this world in a new body.

Once Mr Pinkie got going, he talked for great lengths about many things. He was a gentle and knowledgeable man who could not understand his wife's desire to go and live in a land of 'yellow heads'; hence the divide between them grew. As we got ready for bed Pinkie left to go and sleep in her room at the other end of the street whilst Mr Pinkie shared his bed with his daughter. When they came to say goodnight to us they spotted some bottles of beer on the shelf above the bed. Chastising themselves for not being good hosts they pressed them upon us. Tim and I sat squished in a tiny single bed, drinking beer through newly brushed teeth. It was freezing cold but we were in a home, a clean, loved and looked after home. We were alone. That night I was relaxed enough to make love.

The first person to get a cup of tea in the morning was the Dalai Lama. The cup sat before his picture for a full ten minutes before it was poured out to us.

My bowels had still not sorted themselves out; I was suffering from shooting pains in my colon that for the last few nights had kept me awake. I did not want to venture off to the wild hills of Meghalaya without first checking that everything was as it should be. Pinkie took me to the local doctor.

The surgery was a wooden shack with a pharmaceutical counter at the front and rows of benches where the patients sat clutching a numbered ticket. Across the street was another surgery with the sign: 'F.S.Roy, Dentist and Vet.' I suppose that was what you call a talented man. I think we had come to the Shillong equivalent of Harley Street as every other shack had some medical association. The one that was the most disturbing had a placard outside: 'Blood, Urine, Sputum, Stool, Semen Tested Here.'

It did not take me long to realise that there was some crafty queue-barging going on. As the patient left the next number was called out from behind the curtain. When it was number fourteen's turn four men got up and shuffled into the cubicle. Trying to ascertain what was going on I watched the four pairs of feet in the gap between the curtain and the floor. There was muffled talking and then one of the pairs of feet disappeared. There followed some coughing and slapping and more talking. The second man's trousers then fell around his ankles followed by a lot of hearty giggles - the downside of having a mass diagnosis.

When it was my turn, Tim, Pinkie and I squeezed into the cubicle. The doctor's eyes lit up at the sight of us, he bowed and scraped and treated me with utter reverence. I was diagnosed as having some sort of colonic infection caused by eating contaminated food but it didn't sound too serious. Clutching a bag of virulent-looking pills we left just as three men entered the cubicle. Perhaps this wasn't some time saving device; maybe they had all visited the local fancy woman and had come to compare their ravaged members.

It was time to go on a fact-finding mission and to let the Chief of Police and District Commissioner know of our intended travel plans. By late afternoon we had met all the local government bigwigs. With Pinkie and the raucous Tenzings in tow we schlepped from the District Commissioner's office to the Chief of Police, to the Head of the Forestry Department and, finally, to the Chief Engineer - a move which resulted in a taste of what lies behind Indian bureaucracy.

'Where are your visitors' permits?' barked the Superintendent.

'Um…we don't need them anymore. The state government abolished the need for permits two years ago.'

News travels slowly up here. It soon became apparent that each chief felt nervous about giving their total benediction, so instead would palm us off to their colleague of another department.

'The problem is you see, I am not responsible for that particular area. You must go and see…'

And so it continued.

Indian government offices are one and all alike, cavernous and dreary buildings with peeling paint and loitering figures. The corridors are lined with ante-chambers full from floor to ceiling with manila files. It is like being in a padded cell; one could ricochet off stacked shelves into shoulder-height piles of them without ever coming into contact with furniture. By contrast, the boss's office is empty save for an enormous forbearing desk with a nasty plastic desk set and one manila file. Our request for permission to stay in government buildings was scribbled down on a flimsy sheet of paper, put into the manila file then handed over to the clerk to be added to the ever mutating heap in one of the ante-chambers. I was not over confident that it would reach the right people in time.

The Deputy Chief of Police tapped out our route with a big stick on the map hanging on the wall. He advised us to bypass certain villages because of militant disturbances, to reach each destination by dusk and, as much as possible, contact every local police station on the way to let them know we were in the area. The overall reaction from everyone was disbelief; they were bewildered that this cycling cohort from England wanted to pedal around their isolated hills. There were no temples to visit, no holy ghats, no fancy hotels, just hills and simple villages. Well, there was their answer.

Back in Sewerhati we collected the bikes and found another hotel for the night. When I was a child the second most boring thing in the world after any car journey lasting longer than fifteen minutes was hanging around a hotel lobby whilst my father checked us in. He worked abroad so this was quite a common occurrence. My impatience at the endless filling-in of forms lessened slightly as I got older until I came to India. Every hotel had ledgers the size of the Doomsday Book; they wanted your father's name, the name of your local police station, what diseases you had and how much you earned. To leave a box empty was not good enough.

'Please sir, what is to be your local police station?'

'Paddington Green.'

'Pad...dingtongreen. Ah, I am thinking it is a very nice name sir.'

At the end of a long day it took our last ounce of energy to remain composed especially as at the end of the palaver you could guarantee a couple of cockroaches would appear in your room just to test your patience that little bit more.

The night before we left for Meghalaya I couldn't breathe, I had a sense of foreboding that I couldn't put into words. Tim soothed my fears and tried to inject me with a sense of excitement. We were in for a trip of a lifetime, what we had experienced so far was mandatory for India; this was going to be something special. We would be cycling through places where the locals have never seen a white face before, a race of headhunters who up until a few years ago displayed human skulls in their huts. Exactly! I wished with all my might that we were going to Goa!

'One often becomes what he believes himself to be.
If I keep on saying to myself that I cannot do a certain
thing, it is possible that I may end by really becoming
incapable of doing it.   On the contrary, if I have a belief
that I can do it, I shall surely acquire the capacity to do
it even if I may not have had it at the beginning.'

Mahatma Gandhi

8
INTO THE BOONIES

A certain degree of mental preparation is needed to accomplish a one hundred and twenty-five kilometre ride on rough roads, with dusty heat and a heavy bicycle. Our saving grace was that the first day's ride was flat. What I found to be fatal was looking at the computer after only riding for half an hour; after subtracting eighteen measly kilometres I might as well have poured molten lead into my legs. Sometimes the only way to describe it was boring; hour after hour of monotonous peddling when the only thoughts filling my head was of arriving at my destination.

Our long cycle rides were turning out to be meditations in themselves. Every day posed the problem of finding the right balance between constant energy and focus of mind. Without focus I found the days passed in twitchy desires, I often became irritable and my head reeled with hectic thoughts. My suffering was an inability to succumb, to stop fighting the boredom and the fatigue and to stop myself from wishing that I were anywhere but in the present.

But gradually I did begin to feel myself change, the constant chattering in my head subsided slightly and I enjoyed glimpses of stillness. It felt like parts of me were being emptied, the stagnant dross of past worries and disappointments mulched up in the waste disposal unit that was my bicycle. My yoga teacher at home talked of form as emptiness and emptiness as form, a metaphysical expression that had always left me rather flummoxed. Spending day after day on my saddle I felt I was beginning to understand what that meant. My expectations of the day were less and my restlessness became more subdued. My structure felt hollow allowing space to fill up with the sights and sounds immediately around me. I found I could give my full attention to the jewellery seller who rode beside us or to the smell of the passing river or to the jangling of the cowbells. How then could I ever think this boring when each second trumpeted a juggernaut of life? For the first time in years my lungs allowed me to take huge inhalations, my corset of tension was weakening at the seams, my fist of consternation had gently begun to soften.

We tended to cycle for forty kilometres or so before stopping for breakfast. Lee was rather bombastic in the science of carbo-loading but I found the biggest motivation was an empty stomach and the thought of a good nosh-up. It took a while to release the idea of a honey and muesli style breakfast when all there was were *puris* and variations on a spicy vegetable curry. *Puris* are flat circles of dough that puff up when put in bubbling fat. They are served fresh from the primus stove with little bowls of curry and are delicious.

The more basic the shack, the more fantastic the food. I had managed to dispel my neuroticism and was now able to wolf back whatever was put before me, even drinking the water from the jugs on the table. We might as well have had 'We have loads of rupees and eat like pigs' emblazoned on our T-shirts. They hovered by us, filling up our bowls at any opportunity whilst the *puri* man engrossed himself in a frenzy of frying.

My favourite eateries were the ones decorated with newspaper clippings of Bollywood. I learned nuggets of worthwhile information about the worshipped stars of the 'Masala Movies'. For instance the up-and-coming star of the Indian equivalent, 'The Wallah, The Singh, The Rajput and His Lover', demanded nothing other than barbecued chicken in his lunch box. No whim of the stars would be too great for the studio moguls to satisfy, after all fifteen million people go to the movies every day. They make over eight hundred films a year and hold the world box-office record. One cinema showed the same film for five years. It is not uncommon for an actress or actor to have made three hundred films during his or her career. Overkill is obviously not an issue in India. One actress filmed three movies simultaneously, putting in three shifts a day on each of the films, zooming from one studio to the next with an impressive entourage.

The adoration for stars and directors became apparent whenever a catastrophe or death occurred. When one famous actor was seriously injured on a set, his house was surrounded by thousands keeping vigil. One female fan even went to the lengths of walking backwards for three hundred miles in penance so that his life might be saved. When the movie maker Satyajit Ray died, India came to a standstill and 600,000 people poured onto the streets of Calcutta in homage for all that he had done for Indian cinema.

The common thread between the male stars was the fixation with their hair-dos. I am sure many a western man with a thinning pate could appreciate this preening but to me their sex appeal went down a few notches. How could a woman begin to compete? Love of hair did not only apply to the film stars. During a tea stop in a busy market-place I watched a newly coiffured chap sitting in a barber's chair. For a full twenty minutes he did not take his eyes away from his reflection, slowly rotating his head to marvel at his left profile and then his right. Just to make sure that he was indeed gorgeous, he repeated it again, this time with the chin ever so slightly lowered.

The men's sexuality puzzled me. Everywhere you looked men walked hand in hand or lolled together with entangled arms. And what about the painted fingernails? Homosexuality is illegal in India and couples caught in the sexual act could be subjected to life imprisonment. Most gay men, therefore, remain in the closet or go to Mumbai, which is the only place that has a real gay scene. If one is not allowed to get close to a woman until the dowry has been safely handed over and if homosexuality is strictly taboo then physical contact must be had from somewhere, why not from the weight of your best friend's arm about your shoulder?

By dusk we had to have reached a place called Dainadubi just on the borders of Assam and Meghalaya. If the flimsy piece of paper in the manila file at Shillong had been dealt with then a Forestry Inspection bungalow would be waiting for us.

After about eighty kilometres of keeping up a steady pace of twenty-seven kilometres per hour, my knees were really beginning to suffer. Lee cycled up to me and studied my action for a while.

'Yes, well that's because you are not maximising your strength. Your use of the gears is all wrong, you need lighter gears and need to pedal faster.'

Am I doomed to be told I have a bad technique with everything that I undertake?

We arrived at the junction at Dudnoi, the last town of any proper size before turning off to Dainadubi. It was getting late in the day and we wanted to check the distance left to ride; previous experience had taught us not to rely too heavily on map calculations. The two traffic policemen told us thirty-two kilometres; the shopkeeper said fifteen kilometres; the Mr Know-It-All on the street corner was emphatic, he silenced the gathering rabble and declared with more authority than anyone else, 'I am thinking it is definitely seven kilometres sir.' Oh Lord! We thought we would take the mean distance.

The road petered out to be replaced by a rough track strewn with fist-sized boulders that played havoc with our wheels. It took our last ounces of strength to keep our bicycles vertical; in comparison the Siddhartha Highway seemed positively smooth. Seven kilometres had long since passed, Mr Know-It-All didn't really know it all, at all. The light was beginning to fade. If the shopkeeper was right, then we had eight more kilometres to go. We stepped up the pace. My feelings of foreboding returned with added weight, I knew that our grandiose plan was anything but foolproof.

The buildings thinned out, the villages got further and further apart from one another. It worried me that our fellow commuters were travelling in the opposite direction to us. They shuffled home in insubstantial sandals, their tools on their backs. Others were on bicycles, negotiating the stones with a lot more success than we were. Everywhere was silent. Lee was far ahead, Tim, a little way in front of me; I could tell by the set of his shoulders and the grim expression on his face when he turned round to check on me that he was having the same misgivings as I was. We hailed Lee down, our voices ringing shrill in the evening quiet. What to do? Our choices were few, either to carry on in the hope that an Inspection Bungalow would materialise - but how to recognise one if we saw it? - or to turn on our heels and go back to Dudnoi and hope to find somewhere to stay there. I was all for turning around, preferring to travel back in the dark rather than going further into the boonies on blind faith alone. The boys thought we should carry on.

Just as we were having our group meeting, a man came up to us on a bicycle. Amongst the babble of Garo, we picked out the words, 'Inspection Bungalow.' He bade us follow him. There was something about him that was not quite altogether, he did not draw breath once and he had a rather demonic look about him. We tried to lose him but he stuck steadfastly to us. The track then left the open fields and he beckoned us into the woods. I gasped, we had entered a silver forest. It looked prehistoric, huge silver leaves shimmered in the last rays of the setting sun, bowing down to graze the path on either side. The smell of woodsmoke filled our nostrils, the trees softly whispered as a gentle breeze shook their branches. We momentarily forgot our plight. We went deeper in until our crazed guide abruptly turned left. There nestled amongst a banana plantation was a Hansel and Gretel bungalow, painted an off-beat green with four smiling men standing to attention on the front veranda.

I was so relieved I wanted to whoop with joy, instead I followed SK Das, the second officer in charge, to our rooms. It was gracious and spotlessly clean. I ran my hand over starched white sheets, I hung my clothes over an antique clothes-horse. The mosquito net billowed down, pristine and intact. Buckets of water, albeit cold, had been laid out for us in the bathroom, and tea and biscuits awaited us in the drawing room. I felt like a misplaced Karen Blixen.

We sat down for tea in the drawing room while our supper was being prepared. One by one various officers of the Forestry Department arrived bringing their offspring with them so that we could sit and listen to their scholastic achievements. SK Das, who was an immigrant Bengali, was the most gushing.

'My son, he is the top of maths in whole of Meghalaya and he is speaking Garo like his mother tongue.'

The three of us made the appropriate noises of admiration before turning to listen to the others. Indians would sacrifice everything if it meant that their children could be properly educated. What we see as our birthright they view as an opportunity.

Amongst us six different languages were being spoken and with varying degrees of clarity. One officer spoke only Khasi, the other Hindi with a touch of Garo, another Assamese and Jaintia. SK Das smugly spoke them all, especially English.

'I am speaking English like my mother tongue.'

That was one of SK Das' favourite sayings. At the last census eighteen main languages were counted in India and 1600 minor ones.

The Bengalis were the most connected to the British, so they have an extra affiliation with the language and give a high priority to education.

We painted a courtly picture and it was hard to know which of us was feeling the most unnatural. We sat for hours, wishing the copious amounts of tea would loosen the tongue as much as a glass of beer, as we kept our desire to sprawl our aching limbs in check. The Chief of the Forestry Department was a suave character. He was suave because he had a crew cut - no narcissistic preening for him. He had uprooted his family from the throbbing metropolis of Shillong and deposited them in the middle of the Enchanted Forest, all for his love of trees. I was not surprised to learn they were a little miffed.

The demise of India's forests is a serious polemic whichever way you turn. The problems started during British rule when huge chunks of forests were cut down to build railways and mines. This deforestation had serious ramifications on the tribals whose livelihoods were at stake. They found themselves having to walk further each day to gather fuel and fodder, floods were frequent and the topsoil washed away bringing famine and hunger. The British left but still the timber was extracted at a frightening pace so that now just over ten percent of India's forest cover remains. The government is endeavouring to redress the situation but insufficient funds make it a slow and dispiriting task.

So much of India's culture seems to be entrenched in her forests and, just as water represents the path where a spirit would cross over to the shores of wisdom, so is a tree still believed to be sacred. Over the hills in Nagarland you would find trees with names. When a child is born a tree is planted and given the same name as the child. The tribals look to the tree as a provider - a source of food, materials for housing, tools and music and fuel. As the child and tree grow up so a strong bond develops and, as both blossom into maturity, the young adult knows that the tree will look after him, if he looks after the tree.

Hindus believe that the trees are the heart and lungs of the earth. So important are they that Indian cities are designed around the geometry of a tree. At the centre of every city lies a grove of trees from which the streets radiate out like branches. This reminds the city dweller that whilst they are fulfilling their material role in life, when that stage is over they should retreat to the woods to end their days in quiet contemplation and meditation. The trees teach them tolerance and patience, to bear all difficulties like they bear severe cold and scorching heat without complaint. Buddha found enlightenment under a tree, Krishna learnt to worship nature and reams of religious and ecological texts were inspired from the ever regenerative and self-sufficient bodies of the forests.

Stories of tree heroics were two-a-penny but one that stood out was an epic Joan of Arc tale of martyrdom. A Bishnoi tribal woman called Amrita Devi clung to a tree in an attempt to protect the forests surrounding her village from a group of axemen sent from the king's palace nearby. As the axe was held aloft she begged and pleaded for them to respect their faith which forbade any of the trees to be cut down. She was coldly ignored and as her body was spliced in two she cried, 'A chopped head is still easier to replace than a chopped tree.' As the felled tree, stained with the blood of Amrita Devi, thundered to the ground her daughter took her place. The same fate awaited her, as it did her younger sister and the next sister after that, who all died as they clung to their trees. News of the bloodshed spread throughout the neighbouring villages whereupon men and women took up the cause to protect their forests. The axemen continued until nightfall when three hundred and sixty people had died. When the king heard of the massacres he vowed never again to cut down the Bishnoi trees.

I found it easy to listen to these stories, always fantastical, sometimes preposterous but never dull. However, certain facts had to be gleaned from our friends so we could prepare ourselves for our onward journey. The question burning on all of our lips was for how long would the road remain in this condition?

'Only nine more kilometres of stones and then black topping.' assured one senior officer. SK Das, who had no qualms about undermining his officers in charge, was a stickler for detail.

'Excuse me sir, but I think you are wrong in this matter, you will find I am right, it is eight and a half kilometres of stones and then black topping.'

His statements were always followed by the same movements, a physical exclamation mark, arms crossed, eyes closed, wobble-wobble of the head and then chin pulled sharply down as if to say, 'end of story.' We were told to take the left fork in the road which would take us on to Williamnagar where they would get a message to the PWD (Public Works Department) to put us up in the bungalow there. We had to pass through a village called Songsak, which is the Garo extremists' headquarters and had recently been the scene of some ambushes. They made us promise that we would check in at the local police station on arrival in the village.

One by one they left for their own homes in the woods apart from SK Das who fussed over us like a mother hen, ushering us through into the dining room where a table was groaning with food. At last we could relax but we ate in silence, too drained and too exhausted to make conversation. We could hear the two cooks talking softly in the backyard, the hum of the crickets and not much else. We felt a million miles away from anywhere.

As I lay next to Tim that night I did a countdown in my head of how many more nights we had together. I found myself slipping into an old boarding school mechanism that took me back twenty years, as vivid and real as when I was nine years old. I would divide my school holiday into three categories – no dread, semi-dread and major dread. For instance, the Easter holiday lasted for three weeks, so for the first week every night when I climbed into bed I told myself that I had no cause for concern, I could go to sleep happily knowing that I still had twenty-four more sleeps to go.

In the second category, the same carefree feelings could be attached to the first part of the week but towards the end, bedtime became a little less attractive as I knew my departure was looming. I ruined my final week, so intent was I on labelling everything: the last trip to the supermarket with Mum, the last Saturday bonfire with Dad, the last supper (which took on sacrosanct proportions), until it was time to put my trunk in the car and leave the idyll of Tiger House.

It wasn't so much that I hated school, it was more that I dreaded those ghastly few minutes of saying goodbye. For the last few days before my departure I held on to my mother's skirt at every opportunity, my hot hand leaving a fist-sized patch of crease marks. I dreaded waiting for the multitude of kisses to be delivered on my damp cheeks before they drove down the drive back into the outside world. I remember standing at the gate for several minutes blinking back the tears and feeling like I had swallowed a cabbage.

Twenty years later, lying in the dark next to the man I loved, I found myself imagining our final goodbye. How I curse my emotional memory! It made me feel sick and hot and clammy until I placated myself that I was still in category one - no cause for sadness yet, I still had twenty more sleeps with him. I woke Tim up to tell him about my dread of goodbyes. He was astounded at my capacity to ruin the here and now with such disabling fears for something that will inevitably happen. I tried to explain to him that the stronger the emotion, the deeper the mark it impacts upon the mind. I guess, for all my protestations for living in the present, I still had a long way to go.

A few days later I came across a verse in the *Rig Veda* - the sacred text of Hinduism:

"Two Birds with fair wings, knit with bonds of friendship,
In the same sheltering tree have found a refuge.
One of the twain eats the Figtree's fruitage;
The other, eating not, regardeth only."

It was explained to me that the birds in the Tree of Life show the two realms existing in ourselves. The bird eating the figs signifies the probing, fumbling side of existence, a life driven by desires and fears, likes and dislikes, so that when both awake and dreaming it never rests, plagued by a constant stream of discursive thought. The bird who looks on but refrains from gorging is our pure consciousness which does not argue or weigh the pros and cons, it is our own natural instinct far removed from critical appraisal and it is therefore what we could call our true judgement.

It was all very well to understand but I knew that when my bird was hungry a dozen wild horses could not drag it away from a laden fig tree.

The next morning more bowls of curry and plates of *roti* awaited us. Something strange had happened to Lee overnight, he looked a peculiar shade of green. We knew things weren't as they should be, Lee never skimped on a chance to do some important carbo-loading. Before we left SK Das organised a photo opportunity in front of the house with the houseboys, cooks and Mrs. SK Das who was not speaking English like her mother tongue. For his final act of benevolence he handed us each a packed lunch wrapped up in a banana leaf.

'I am thinking there is no place for fooding or drinking on the way, you must fill up your water bottles at the police station.'

We paid our bill, all the time SK Das apologising for having to charge us but he had to pay the houseboys and cover the cost of the food. The bill came to fifty pence each.

*"I soon realised that no journey carries one far unless,
as it extends into the world around us, it goes an equal
distance into the world within."*

Lillian Smith

9
FREE ESCORT SERVICE

We bumped out of the Enchanted Forest into a cloud of thick, billowing smoke. On the other side lay enticing stretches of black topping, but first we had to get through the road-surfacing barricade. The workers froze mid-task. We had learnt the very basics of Garo in an attempt not to appear so alien. In a happy and friendly fashion we sang out our greetings; their faces didn't register. I have never seen such crude tools. The women's job was to level the road, on hands and knees they scraped the road flat with old flip-flops, whilst the men stirred the tar in an oversized wok.

We reached the black topping and in an instant we took-off. Save for one or two trucks we had the road to ourselves, and what a road it was too. It dipped and rose, veered round corners, along rivers, through valleys and up hills with thickets of bamboo on either side. Exotic bushes dripped with chlorophyll and glorious butterflies skittered alongside us. The quietness and space was insurmountable.

At first it was imperceptible, gradually becoming stronger and stronger until I was in danger of asphyxiation. I knew I had encountered the smell of the Garo hills somewhere before but I wracked my brains to make the connection. In the dry heat it bounced off the road and clung to the trees driving me slightly crazy. I suspected it was related to my childhood. Later in the day, as I was freewheeling down a hill, it came to me at last; it was the smell of baking flour and water paste. With each inhalation I took, a scene from my childhood came back to me: the shaft of sunlight streaming onto the black and white tiles of the kitchen linoleum, me at six years old standing impatiently by the oven.

'Mum, Mum I think it's ready.'

'No darling, another five minutes.'

'Another five minutes!'

In child-time that speaks of eternity, another whole five minutes before my dollshouse fruit bowl and birthday cakes were fully baked. I was astonished at the clarity of my memory, each time I breathed in a new detail came to light: the rabbit and carrot tea-towel hanging on the oven rail, the cut-out magazine articles lying on the slatted mat in the shape of a fish, the rogue peanut lying between the squash cupboard and the fridge; such mundane household items that were a daily part of my life I thought I had long forgotten .

The smell of the Garo hills had spontaneously invoked an unremarkable incident in my life with awesome definition. I felt as if a time machine had been inserted under my skin so that as long as this smell persisted I could live in two dimensions, switching from being six to twenty-nine with something so fantastically simple as breathing in.

Every twenty kilometres or so we encountered tiny bamboo villages untouched by time, carved out of the hillside and surrounded by glistening rice fields. The bamboo turned out to be unsuspectingly hazardous. Lying across the road like a cattle grid was stem after stem of bamboo. The reason for this was ingenious; the tribals make their houses out of bamboo and by laying them across the road they get flattened by passing trucks thus allowing them to be woven into the structure for the houses.

Each house was woven into a different pattern. Some were so fancy as to have three different types of weave. The main bulk of the wall was a tight pattern, the windows more diamond-shaped allowing for ventilation and a porthole design underneath the thatch. Not one nail or screw is used, everything is tied together with strong grasses. We were not of much help in the flattening process and judging by the number of trucks we had passed that day, it must be a lengthy business.

As we cycled through the villages young children ran crying to their mothers. We shouted out our greeting, giving huge smiles and waves, but nothing would placate them, so strange we must have appeared. The adults stood by, the older ones staring in vague recognition, the brave ones grinning from ear to ear and shouting something back in reply.

We turned left at the one and only junction and the black topping finished. For two hours we bumped and skidded along, the concentration needed to stay upright on the saddle was exhausting and my feelings of foreboding returned again. After my third tumble of the day I limped into the village where we had promised to check in at the local police station. It was market day and the place was humming. First things first though, a restorative cup of tea was in order. We set our bikes outside the tea shack which were immediately surrounded by all of the village children and then ventured inside.

Everywhere we looked there were women: women chatting, handling babies, having a kip or enjoying a favourite pastime – chewing *paan*. We couldn't see one man except for the lucky one who served us. So this is what is meant by a matriarchal society. It made a nice change from the villages of Europe where it is the men who while away the day in inconsequential leisure. The women looked haughty and slightly stoned. What they didn't look was Indian. As we sipped our tea the shack filled up until every inch of bench space was taken. They stared at us, we stared at them. We got up to go, so did they. Finn was right, they were pygmies, they only came up to our shoulders.

We picked our way through the market stalls that comprised mostly of cauliflowers and *paan*. In the northeast the people love *paan*, everywhere you look the ground resembles a Jackson Pollock masterpiece of red spittle. Prolonged use can cause mouth cancer and in the meantime ravages the gums and teeth. The upside is that it enhances life, the effects inducing a mild buzz. It is a stimulant that imbues the chewer with a feeling of euphoria. No wonder the women in the teahouse looked stoned.

Paan is the word for a betel nut concoction, a cocktail of a vine leaf, lime paste, pieces of betel nut and an assortment of added extras depending on the individual's tastes. The leaf comes from the betel vine, the greener and fresher the better. To destroy any bacteria that might be on the leaf lime paste is smeared over it. The chopped or sliced betel nut is then added plus extras which could be anything from opium, ginger or cumin seeds or flavoured tobacco. It is then wrapped up into a little pocket and popped in the mouth between the gums and the cheek. The first few moments of chewing are hard work until the leaf and the nut become malleable. The chewing stimulates a flow of red saliva, the juices seep into the system and the hard pieces of wood are eventually spat out.

Paan has been chewed for ten thousand years and the varying attributes have been many. In ancient times it was believed to be cleansing and strengthening. Some thought it aided the expulsion of wind, others that it quelled body odour and even killed worms. It is also considered to have lustful properties hence its nickname, 'bed-breaker.' Perhaps that explains why every woman and every little girl decorate the roadside with babies balanced on jutted hips.

We were running a couple of hours behind schedule because of our snail's pace on the awful road. The day was boiling and by the time we located the police station we were covered in dust and felt light-headed with dehydration. We checked in and were given directions to the next Inspection Bungalow and continued with the battle of black-topping versus short cut. Time was not on our side; we had to ride through the unsavoury village of Songsak well before nightfall if we did not want to encourage unnecessary problems. Lee's health had taken a downward turn and we were all physically shattered. If we took the pitch road it would cut our journey by twenty kilometres, a very enticing option, but we knew that the remaining thirty would be hell. Now was not the time to take the road less travelled, we thought we should get onto the tarmac and put our heads down. If we maintained a speed of twenty-five kilometres per hour we would be in Williamnagar by 5.00pm. Where was my James Bond device when I needed it?

For once I was in the lead, probably because Lee was ill and Tim said he wanted to enjoy the view of my backside. Regardless, I felt like Boadicea, I was eating up the kilometres so intent was I on getting to Williamnagar by nightfall.

We had been going for half an hour when a jeep hared past us full to bursting with combat-geared policemen brandishing rifles. Three of them were standing up, the flaps of their dust scarves streaming out behind them. Six others were hunched down furtively scanning the countryside. Not even a black Capri could boast the testosterone levels pumping out of that jeep. They had an air of emergency about them and looked like they meant business. Perhaps trouble was afoot in Songsak? We continued on our way until we came across them again, pulled over on the side of the road. We recognised the chief officer and waved. We kept up the pace, the sun was beginning to sink and we still had a fair way to go.

Quarter of an hour later the jeep sped past again and sure enough we duly overtook them a few minutes later. We waved and smiled, they put their heads down. It did not take a brain surgeon to work out that they had supplied us with our very own escort, although for some reason they did not want to make it look obvious. I am afraid that never in a million years could they ever get away with being described as under-cover. I didn't know whether it was a comfort or not. Was this just an excuse to liven up their day, or did the situation really warrant our protection? It all seemed vaguely surreal. I am not one of the five percent of the population who actively seek out excitement in such an intrepid fashion. I suddenly rather wished I was at home.

The road went through a forest, the flour and water smell still as evocative, the black topping evasive once more. Just before Songsak we heard some distant rumbling. The sound was a cavalcade of lorries, perhaps twenty of the clumbering beasts. We dismounted and edged ourselves as close to the side as possible as they rumbled past us spewing up loathsome amounts of dust which clung to our sweaty bodies and made us choke. The green forest turned a seventies-lounge brown in an instant and we drew tribal markings on our faces.

As we entered Songsak our escort ditched its attempt to remain inconspicuous and positioned itself up our behinds. Nothing looked particularly untoward. The villagers were just as smiley, the pace equally as sleepy and there did not seem to be any subversive operations taking place. We cycled past the police station where our escort stopped and another one took its place. We were feeling more important by the minute.

Without a doubt one of the worst things about cycling is an unexpected hill, especially if it hits you at the end of the day. Before we set off each morning we would scour the map not only for directions but for the number of climbs, straight legs and downhill stretches. This meant that a certain amount of physical, not to mention mental pacing could be done. When a climb sneaked up out of the blue I took it as a huge personal affront, inspiring such violent feelings that I ended up hating the country, hating Tim for putting me through this in the first place and hating myself for wasting valuable energy in prima donna expostulations. The unfairness of life (note how easy it was to lose perspective) was marginally alleviated by a good bout of swearing either to Tim or to anything on which I could vent my displeasure.

'You shit, you wanker! Tim, I am not bloody getting on a bicycle ever again after this! Find yourself another sodding girlfriend.'

The fickleness of women – once at the top with the thought of whizzing down the other side, suddenly everything was roses once more. I whooped with elation, 'Tim, I love yooooouuuuuu.'

On this particular occasion the situation was too grim to even bother with such expletives; out of the blue loomed an enormous hill. Lee was ashen, his health fading fast along with his mood. In Lee's eyes it was inexcusable that Tim, who was map reader that day, had miscalculated the hill. Tim argued it was hardly the standard of an Ordnance Survey map, so how was he supposed to know that a couple of concentric circles translated into a bloody great climb? Our mood was not congenial.

Even our trusted escort had given up on us; they had long passed, probably rather deflated that their valuable assignment had turned out to be such a non-event. Just as the last rays of sun sank behind a yonder hill we reached the top, sweating and panting. We heard voices and saw licks of flames shooting up into the darkening sky. It looked like our escort had waited for us. There were a few surly nods from the policemen, which turned me rather paranoid. I felt a strong need to apologise.

'I am sorry we're so slow, we've had a long day, Lee's not well, the roads...God, I am ever so sorry, you all must be very tired and not to mention bored...'

The boys told me to shut up! Well I didn't know how to deal with nine policemen on a mission to look after us? It is hardly a regular occurrence in west London. Suitably silenced I put on my dynamo and warm clothes ready for the downhill run.

The whole experience was horrific. The colour of the sky was going through each HB pencils number, the prelude to the inevitable charcoal. The beam from my light, for some inexplicable reason, produced barely a glow so I had to ride as close behind Tim as was feasibly safe. The road caught us unawares with large potholes nearly throwing us from our bikes. My body was rigid with fear, insects flickered across my face and I could not stem my continual whimpering. I thought it was only a matter of time before the next ditch threw me crashing to the floor. On and on we went, the lowlands not seeming to get any nearer, Tim relaying the road conditions to us from the front.

'Hole! Rock! Bridge!' Until a short while later, 'Hole! Rock! Shit! SHIT! **SHIT!** Can you believe it? I have a bloody puncture.'

Oh Christ, if there couldn't be a worse time to get a puncture. The escort jeep stopped behind us and the policemen trundled out and gathered around Tim who was furiously throwing his panniers from his bike. I shuffled from one foot to the other, shining my torch on Tim and using the occasion to have a proper look at our bodyguards. Far from looking exasperated each face was animated, after all, this was the first bit of excitement we had given them.

Tim can turn the process of changing a tyre into poetry in motion. A brief stint as a cycle courier means that he can hold his own in the pit stop of any biking equivalent of Formula 1. But now that he had an audience of riveted beefcakes he flunked the procedure good and proper. Lee joined in but still the tyre would not come off the rim. We had now succeeded in losing any ounce of credibility we may have had. A few of them came to the rescue headbutting Tim with their rifles as they bent down to help him. I began to get the giggles, so ludicrous was the situation. For fear of exacerbating Tim's wrath I turned away from the mirthless scene, my eyes falling upon a wooden church sitting contentedly on a green. It was aglow with epiphanal light and my ears caught the strains of hymns echoing out into the night. I found that if I squinted my eyes I could almost think I was in Lower Warbleswick.

We had been told that this part of the sub-continent was home to a high percentage of Christians, the gathering arms of missionaries scooping up these tribespeople and declaring them children of God. I wondered if their prayers to Jesus were different to the ones they may have chanted to Buddha or to the Hindu gods and goddesses. Instead of striving to sweep away all impurities from the heart by studying the *Vedas*, now they were hoping to have a direct experience with God through evangelical devotion.

Here we were in the West, thrashing around in a spiritual crisis harbouring mistrust in the religious and social structures attached to Christianity beginning to look more and more to the ancient philosophies of the East. We want our perceptions and intellect to take on a different perspective. We hope for some sort of transcendence that will appease our spiritual vacuum and replace our disenchantment of material values and self-seeking survival. One only has to look at the overflowing shelves in the Mind, Body, Spirit section of any bookstore to know that somewhere along the line something has gone terribly wrong.

I speak for myself and for my friends, who to all extents and purposes are living the life we dreamed of when we were little. By day we work at being successful in our chosen careers, by night we buzz around the city looking young and beautiful, sipping Sea Breezes on black leather stools and kicking off designer shoes as we talk of anti-aging serums and how to make a million. Yet we come home and pad aimlessly about our flats. The frenetic adrenaline of the day is over and we find ourselves staring detachedly at our stylish gismos and our testaments to a fulfilled life: the invitations, the postcards, the photos. Our hearts race with anxiety and fear. All we want to do is to sit for a moment on our sofas enjoying a feeling of peace and reflection at the end of the day. We don't though, we can't, we're too twitchy. Instead we bleakly dab our faces with expensive cream and curl up under the duvet wondering what on earth it could be that is making us feel so lonely and unhappy.

And then a leaflet is thrust into our hand as we exit the tube station. In bold letters at the top it reads: "DEPRESSED? ANXIOUS? DO YOU SUFFER FROM STRESS RELATED ILLNESSES, INSOMNIA, FEELINGS OF PANIC? If you answer 'yes' to any of these questions then you could benefit from Transcendental Meditation." Or other such promises of life changing courses. We have read that William Hague relies on TM, that Goldie Hawn stays young and energetic by doing Power Yoga, that Sting can make love for twelve hours through Tantric intercourse. We think this could be an answer. We sign up for a course rather furtively, worried what our friends may think of our 'Rolfing' session or our hypnotherapy.

'Polly, what are you doing Wednesday night?'

'Oh, I think I'm going home to my parents. My aunt is down from Scotland and well, you know, I had better go and show my face.'

Meanwhile we skulk down dubious looking streets until we find the venue that promises to free our clogged meridians by sticking needles into our sternums. We keep quiet about it for a couple of weeks until over a dinner and a second bottle of wine the floodgates open. To our astonishment we learn that we are not alone. As I was sitting in Lotus in some village hall to relieve my panic attacks, Steph had been going for craniosacral therapy in the hope of redressing a traumatic birth. Billy is learning Reiki, Leo visits a psychic, Mark spends weekends learning how to re-educate his inflicted conditioning. As we swap our stories and experiences it brings about a new dilemma - perhaps Mark's course will bring peace and contentment faster than my sessions of Shiatsu massage? So desperate are we to dispel our unease that we trustingly attach ourselves to any charismatic guru. It is hard to say whether any profound change has taken place. It is certainly easy to be cynical - our bank balances are frighteningly lower and our bookshelves more crowded with 'How to' books.

But what does this mean? Every day new generations of people are growing up mistrustful of religion. We are also aware that we cannot look to science, as perhaps once we might, to answer all our questions. We know there are forces greater than ourselves, we know we cannot quantify the supernatural or continue to believe that time only exists on a linear scale. But as long as we live in the western world our two sides will be at loggerheads. Our ambitious, desiring half continues to whisper in our ear, perhaps life could be better... what if... is this all... is this it? Our other half searches for acceptance, to understand the pain of existence and in doing so enjoy moments when the world seems infinite, and our place in it harmonious. But the wonderful thing about it is, as our Yoga teachers and therapists assure us, once you're on the path of spirituality, or reality, or even morality (whatever word does not make you baulk) then there is never any turning back. This is certainly true and although we now realise the wonder of the path of life, it fails to make it any easier to tread.

Standing in the shadows of the church I wondered what the people of the Garo hills were praying for inside. Their problems were poor sanitation, disease, the right weather to nourish their crops, their hills to be safe once more. What I could be certain of was that no one was praying for a respite from panic attacks or bouts of depression. I did not want them to envy me my western lifestyle, thinking that wealth brought the end of suffering. Instead I envied them their sense of community.

The tyre fixed we set off on the final leg to Williamnagar. I no longer felt scared, each cell of my body was vibrating with exhilaration. The night was now charcoal. The road flattened out and we sped over little bridges cycling faster and faster. My confidence in the darkness grew. I felt more alive then ever.

The town authorities knew we were coming but as regards our accommodation, the right phone calls to the appropriate people had not been made, nor the flimsy bit of paper in the manila file added to the right tower. I can't say I was overly surprised. There was no SK Das waiting to feed our hungry bellies, no welcoming band of smiling faces. Instead we were taken to a Government Circuit House which was more along the lines of a grotty youth hostel in Weston-Super-Mare. We said goodbye to our guards who stuck with us right to the bitter end. They hovered around us, waiting their turn to shake our hands and say thank you. I think we had underestimated the break from the humdrum we gave them. They seemed in no hurry to go home, their stern faces of a few hours ago replaced with beaming smiles now that their important roles were over.

We had two enormous rooms of dubious interior decoration, a mish-mash of floral sofas and laminated coffee tables. We asked the man in charge if there was anything to eat.

'I am sorry, it is not possible.'

'Is there anywhere in the town to get some food?'

'I am sorry, it is not possible.'

'Perhaps a cup of tea?'

'I am sorry, it is not possible.'

This was reminiscent of "Dangerous Liaisons".

'It is beyond my control.'

We fished out all we had in our panniers: two packets of sticky figs, eight Horlicks biscuits and a bunch of bananas. We tried desperately hard not to wolf them down, trying to fashion our larder into some sort of dinner whilst raging hungers raced through our bodies.

Indians do not appear to go in for double beds; since our trip began Tim and I had been sharing a single bed. We were so exhausted at the end of the day that the lack of space was no cause for concern, sleep came too easily. Why is it that, when you want oblivion to hit as soon as possible, an hour can pass in tossing and turning and busy thoughts?

I wanted these precious moments in India to last. We seemed to be racing through our days, always with an agenda to keep and with little time to squander in idle pleasure. The heat of the day, the dust, the physical fatigue was not an inducement to hugs and kisses. Tim's caressing hand could turn me uncharacteristically irascible. At night though, tingling from a cold bucket wash, I wanted to savour our closeness. The cool dampness of his skin, the cuts and burn marks on his hands and forearms appeared to me even more precious now that we were lying together in the middle of nowhere land. I was so full to bursting with love that I wanted to submerge myself into him and to enjoy the playful banter that somehow lying horizontal invites. There was nothing we could do to stop it, two minutes later we were fast asleep.

10

INDIA HERE! BANGLADESH THERE!

Williamnagar turned out to be the town of the red tape. Every building was an office or headquarters for some important organisation or government department. Signs outside the building read: "Office of the Sub-Divisional Senior Deputy Officer of the West Garo Hills Duck Breeding Farms Association." And I am not kidding. Next door a similar looking building painted in the same loo-block turquoise read: "Office of the Executive Officer of the West Garo Hills Duck Breeding Farms Association."

We were becoming rather tired of writing down our details for all and sundry. We could not even have breakfast in peace. Two seedy-looking characters came into the shack where we were enjoying our morning *puris*.

'Please sirs, may I have your details?'

'Why?'

'We are from Special Intelligence.'

They pulled out one scrap of paper from their trouser pocket. It bore no relation to any other piece of paper, nor did it look like it ever would. They rifled agitatedly through our passports and wrote down our Nepal visa details before disappearing on a Vespa. Special Intelligence huh?

Just as we were leaving the town an earnest young man in nylon slacks and a polo-neck hailed us down. With inquiring brown eyes he asked us why we were not going to church that day. We weren't even aware that it was Sunday. We refrained from telling him this, fearing that it would appear even more irreligious than our excuse that we had places to go and people to see.

'But all peoples go to church on Sunday.' A vexed expression crossed his face. 'In your land not all peoples go to church on Sunday?'

'Um…er… no. A lot of them do, yes, but um, not all of them.'

His voice rose a couple of octaves. 'But please sir, you are telling me, what are these peoples doing if they do not go to church on Sunday?'

Why is it that the brothers who speak good English are the ones who are the most moralistic? We nurse our hangovers, go and buy croissants, read what parties the IT girls went to during that week, watch the video we were too pissed to finish the previous night, have sex, put in a load of washing. The list is endless. How could we bombard him with this nonsense? Instead we sympathised.

'I know, let's hope their lost souls find deliverance.'

I was the slowest cyclist known to man that day. I grumbled and groaned through every kilometre. The road was up there on the list of the top five roads I have ever been on in my life but even this did little to mollify my disgruntled demeanour. Pampas grasses sprayed out of the hillside like toothmugs of interdental brushes. The clearest, greenest river bubbled along beside us and clusters of chocolate skin bathed in its waters. Young girls swayed past us balancing ten-foot bamboo poles on their heads, 'chicks with sticks' as Tim called them. It was a bewitching road and still redolent of the kitchen at Tiger House.

If only… there I go again… if only there was somewhere I could get a Coke or a Kingsize Mars Bar to spur me up the last hill. We had indulged in gourmet fantasies over breakfast that morning. I was craving grilled goats cheese salad, Ryvitas smeared with Philadelphia and sliced avocado, black pepper and truckloads of chocolate. I now understood the warning of how not to get sick. So many people, having studiously stayed away from western food, come across the seductive word 'PIZZA' written on the menu of a grubby shack in Kalimpong. Fed up with a diet of rice and *dhal* they throw caution to the wind, the images of bubbling cheese and pungent salami just too much for a vegan/vegetarian by default to withstand. One might as well ask a Catholic priest to share a single bed with Pamela Anderson. And so they tuck in trying to ignore the nagging doubt that something didn't quite taste like the Quattro Formaggio in PizzaExpress. They spend the next bus journey throwing up on the roadside.

As we cycled through the village of Rongram a band of policemen flagged us down. They spoke no English but beckoned us to follow them. We gathered that the chief policeman was expecting us. A rather scraggy man appeared out of a house dressed in a white vest and *lunghi* looking agitated but chirpy.

'I have been waiting for you all day and now I have changed into my resting clothings. *Acha, acha* (ok, ok).'

This adding of 'ing' to the end of nouns was killing us. We were taken to the toy police station and left alone for a few moments, giving us the opportunity to snoop. The police station was a wooden hut set in the middle of a yard with several mangy chickens and a lot of dirt. In the corner of the hut was a table and an eclectic range of chairs set around it. I counted four manila files on the shelf - very restrained - and a telephone that only took incoming calls. Stuck on the wall with drawing pins was a hand-drawn neighbourhood crime grid coloured in with felt-tip pens:

CRIMES COMMITTED DECEMBER 1998 - 0
CRIMES COMMITTED JANUARY 1999 - 1.

We had obviously rocked up to a hotbed of felonious activity. We had just set up a self-time photo opportunity when our police officer reappeared in his Sunday best, a dazzling white shellsuit with Officer's Choice emblazoned on the back, his glossy black hair slicked down and a massive smile fixed firmly in place. He was the Garo Hill's answer to James Brown. There followed a stream of houseboys bringing platter upon platter of cakes and tea as we went through all the usual pleasantries. Here was one guy who liked to have a good time. Everything he said was accompanied by gales of laughter. I reckoned even this was quite restrained; I would not have been surprised if he had spun round on his chair, leapt onto the desk and sung 'Like a Love Machine' whilst thrusting his hips provocatively. He was really quite magnificent. We wanted to glean some local information which was not his idea of a good time at all. We asked him the population of his constituency.

'It is impossible to say, every day more peoples are being born. Ha ha ha ha.'

At least that was one less figure to enter through one ear, bypass my brain and then swiftly exit out of the other. I have an appalling sense of spatial awareness, if he was to say 5,000 or 50,000 I would still picture the same density of people. I never fail to be impressed by someone, who upon hearing the population of Chichester, for example, can then comment confidently, 'Ah you surprise me, 700,000 people, that many huh?'

What do they mean, 'That many?' If I was expected to comment I could only hazard a fifty-fifty guess. We asked him if he had a taxing job.

'Very, very hard. All peoples live so far apart, my men have to go and find them in the hills. The Garo people never lock their doors, they are always open.'

This seemed a strange thing to say seeing as any aspirant burglar or murderer could climb through the bamboo-weave windows. James Brown was much more at home being an agent provocateur than a man of the law, with a quick look side to side he leant forward and rasped, 'Beer? Whisky? Betel? Smoke?'

You could call us killjoys for turning down his menu of

stimulants, but we still had to make it to Tura before nightfall. That old chestnut again. Although chocolate still evaded me my blood sugar levels were running high thanks to the six *ras gullas* I had eaten. Our interlude at Rongram police station had cheered me up no end, the twenty odd kilometres to Tura would be a piece of cake.

James and his entourage stood on the rickety steps waving goodbye and making us promise to return when next we were in the area. Did he realise just how remote his part of the world was? I had more chance of turning shopping into an Olympic sport than returning to the village of Rongram.

We cycled through the village that was no different from the previous one or the one before that. We moan at home about every town becoming cloned with the same shops: Boots, WHSmith, Thomas Cook, HMV but Meghalaya could receive the same criticism. They all boast a tea shack with dirt floors and a couple of shaky benches and a few kiosks selling lethal cigarettes, biscuits, packets of flavoured chewing tobacco and some plastic household tat. Laid out on the ground are big sacks of rice and grain; next door are pyramids of oranges, there are the *paan* wallahs and the sari merchants and never any deviations. The only difference from home is that never in a million years could you call Wycombe High Street atmospheric.

We reached Tura with the light still with us and found the police station, this was all beginning to seem like a walk in the park. Yes, it turned out that they were expecting us but first, 'Please to be filling in your name and details.'

Oh God! I tried to deduce why this simple procedure should take so long. First, it must be understood that the Indians love bureaucracy. This is nothing new, it is a worldwide truism along with never trust an Arab or let your sixteen year-old daughter loose on a Greek island. This love goes deeper than merely doing everything by the book, they actually get-off on writing in the goddamned book in the first place.

Tea was ordered from some young scivvy clerk to compliment the officialdom. The fingers of the chief hovered over his assortment of pens before picking the nib that would best facilitate his most beautiful penmanship. You will never find an Indian with slovenly handwriting. Their script, without exception, is elegant and flowery with each loop of the L and sweep of the Y in perfect harmony with one another. Having completed one page of the ledger he would turn the page and stroke the new sheet with a loving caress that one would normally associate with silken thighs. Our passports caused a slight hiccup in the smooth running of the procedure. While not wanting to lose his air of magniloquence he was obviously unsure of what he was actually supposed to be writing down. The passports were handed to his deputy and then to the sub-deputy before we had to intervene and show the appropriate documents.

I would now like to describe our part in this interchange of cultures. Looking back I must say I am not proud of the way we conducted ourselves. Just bring to mind three, grouchy children adopting the sitting positions of a bunch of drunks outside an Odeon cinema. We sat slumped in chairs, our legs flopping open, our heads hanging to one side and a gormless expression on our faces. Add to this a day's worth of dust and sweat, which in my case concentrated at the bridge of my nose giving me a mono-brow more in keeping with a Sicilian peasant than an English rose. Depending on our levels of tedium and our exhaustion we interrupted the silence with big sighs. Once the information was noted all we had to do was sign. It gave me great satisfaction to scrawl my name in an excessively slipshod manner across the page so that my L's carelessly invaded the meticulous line above; yes, I was twenty-nine going on seven.

Tura was a notable town; it had a concert hall, a zoo, rather fancy villas, its own TV station and toast. The following morning Lee had gone to collect his washing which was drying on the back roof of the Circuit House. On passing the kitchen he noticed the chowdikkar cutting a fresh white loaf of bread. He came back into the room.

'Guys, guys, I think we're having toast for breakfast.'

'TOAST,' squealed I.

'TOAST,' shouted Tim.

Within three minutes we had packed our panniers, loaded our bikes and seated ourselves at the table with expectant looks. Sure enough we had toast: toast of sorts anyway. Indian kitchen and tableware is on the basic side, a couple of pans, one knife and a few pots. They don't have ovens but cook on fires that have been sculpted from clay and mud just like the floor and the sideboard. I suppose this is what you call organic, when the life of the kitchen has finished it can return to the earth whence it came. Understandably, they would sooner affiliate deep-fat fryers, juicers and Magimixs with astro-physics than home economics.

But what they do have are ingenious thermos pots as opposed to thermos flasks. Everything goes in them, the lid is screwed on and the curries and rice kept moist and warm for hours. Unfortunately our toast went into them as well. There was no butter to be found in these parts so strong, yellow mustard seed oil was drizzled over instead. The toast was moist and reminded us of last night's cauliflower curry. But let's face it, no one knows about toast like the Brits. The French can wax lyrical about their prissy plaited creations while the Italians, contrary to popular belief, eat ersatz cakes wrapped in crinkly, shiny wrappers for breakfast. One bite and the mouthful disintegrates into a glupey spreadsheet of E numbers.

The only time I have forsaken toast for another breaded option was at boarding school. It was a vocational school with emphasis on dancing and drama rather than science projects and netball. Hence we went through our school days in permanent, excruciating hunger. We were never allowed to put on those charmless layers of adolescent fat brought on by Friday nights spent toasting Mothers Pride and mooning around to Depeche Mode. When we turned thirteen, we were allowed to have a roll instead of a piece of toast on Mondays, Wednesdays and Fridays. This may not sound cause for much excitement but believe you me, those extra grams of flour that went into a roll filled up our abyss of hunger just that little bit more.

The night before, just as we had settled into our room at the Circuit House, the Chief Officer of the West Garo Hills Sub-Divisional Headquarters of the Forestry Department (from here on referred to as Gregory) knocked on the door with his wife and two kids. I was filthy and exhausted. I have come to the conclusion that I prefer to be stared at by men than I do by women. Gregory's wife and his two daughters were blatant in their appraisal and I feared the outcome was not favourable. When their gaze left me for a second I tried desperately to rub away my mono-brow. Fortunately Tim came to my rescue with a damp tissue. Like a loving parent gently chastising their errant child he interrupted the conversation:

'Look at you! Covered in dirt.' He wiped my forehead and cheeks.

'She is usually beautiful!'

Thanks my darling.

Gregory asked if we minded doing a television interview the next morning for the local Tura TV station. I was sure I packed a lipstick somewhere. After breakfast a jeep turned up and out piled the cameras and crew. The presenter was a very glamorous woman dressed in a fetching sari and adorned with quite a few carats of gold. She bossed and ordered everyone around, including us and positioned us up on the rooftop.

It transpired that Gregory, fresh from a game of squash, was going to play the interviewer. The shellsuit phenomena had come late to India but with no less furore; like our friend James Brown, Gregory had also chosen his shellsuit as his favourite mode of dress. The interview went amazingly smoothly save for Gregory's profuse sweating, a constant stream running down his forehead, which he kept having to mop with a towel. After it was over Mrs. Frosty took him aside to berate him.

'*Acha*, what is the worry? All peoples know I am playing squashing.'

We were then filmed out and about, buying food supplies and finally cycling out of the town. Fame for a day.

I think I have failed to stress the importance of Finn's notes. Inside the envelope lay pages from a ripped out exercise book from his previous trip. He had written, in hotch-potch order, the directions, obstacles and general tips on how to survive in the wild hills of Meghalaya. Sometimes it was like trying to decipher a code; it read something like this:

'*Up down, up down, up down, pass tea garden on left, at junction turn...*'

End of page, but where the hell did it follow on? Often we just had to guess. At the beginning of another page it would commence, '*Right following the road until you reach Kaziranga.*' Hey this must be it. WRONG - Kaziranga is in Assam not Meghalaya.

Up until this point our reading of the notes seemed to be taking us in the right direction. It was hard to judge the rate of deterioration from two years ago, or for that matter, improvements, but for the most part Finn's summary of good roads and shocking roads was correct.

That is until the day of the Border Road between Bangladesh and India.

We loaded up with provisions, as the notes told us to because we were going further and further into Nowheresville. As usual we were running late, this time due to our TV appearance. Lee was still feeling queasy and my knee now felt like someone had taken off the bottom half of my leg and put it on back to front. The notes for the day read:

"Once on border road, straight and smooth all the way to Baghmara. May have to wave to Border Control men but __ON NO ACCOUNT STOP!__"

As we cycled out of Tura I had an uneasy feeling about the day. We rode for long periods of time without seeing any signs of civilisation. The silence was resonating around my head and the panoramic view of bush and scrub inspired feelings of claustrophobia as opposed to liberation. Tim and Lee, ahead of me, looked human and vulnerable. The cosiness of their T-shirts and caps in stark contrast to the unforgiving sun and terrain. Not for the first time did I wonder what we were doing. Our pace was painstakingly slow. Lee needed to rest every half-hour but we had to keep going if we didn't want to sleep on the side of the road that night.

We ignored the first sign to Baghmara, as the notes told us to do, and carried on until we found the border road, the road that was supposed to be smooth, flat and direct. The first few kilometres were stunningly beautiful. Long-lashed cows ambled along the roadside, meandering rivers interrupted green plains, copses and bamboo plantations grew neighbourly side by side. The thin, black tarsealed track wound in and out of a rusty, overgrown, barbed wire fence. Perhaps it was only word association but the road had a feeling of importance about it, it hummed with an air of expectancy and underneath the rural façade lay a tangible tension. I found it hard to comprehend that a single track of tarmac was all there was to separate Bangladesh from India.

It was then that I noticed shadowy figures standing behind the trees on the opposite bank of the narrow river. The branches rustled as hollow cheeks and sunken eyes stared at us. Suddenly the air seemed charged and, despite the scorching sun and clear skies, menacing. We all noticed them; behind every tree hovered Bangladeshis waiting for an opportune moment to make the quick sprint across. How many attempts had they undertaken? Was life in Bangladesh so much worse than India? Did they think their bellies would be filled more easily in the abundant hills of Meghalaya? They inched forward to the shelter of the trees nearest the bank, their minds plotting; perhaps we could provide some decoy? I shivered. Pulling our eyes away from the deserters we came face to face with three giants from the Border Security Force – a division of the Indian army. They screamed, they bellowed, they shook their rifles at us. They spat out an incomprehensible stream of Garo, Hindi, Assamese – I don't know what. One guy made sense.

'STOP! INTERNATIONAL BORDER. STOP! INTERNATIONAL BORDER.'

All we could think of were Finn's notes, "*ON NO ACCOUNT STOP!*"

We endeavoured to continue, pedalling faster and faster and smiling at them blithely as if this was normal routine. Not in their eyes it wasn't. They ran after us, their boots slamming down on the tarmac, their rifles banging against their legs. There was no way we could continue.

'What's the problem?' asked Lee.

'PROBLEM? PROBLEM? INTERNATIONAL BORDER. VERY, VERY SENSITIVE.'

'Whoops, sorry! We didn't know it was sensitive. We have permission to come this way from the Chief of Police in Shillong.'

'NO! You must wait.'

We sat on the grass under a tree whilst the soldier with the fierce bark marched off leaving us in the trusted hands of another. We waited and waited and ate all our provisions because there was nothing else to do. Time was moving on and we still had a lot of ground to cover before Baghmara. Eventually he came back and stressed again the importance of the geography of the road again.

'India here! Bangladesh there!' and he pointed to the grass verge two metres away. We were told later that several hundred people die each year trying to cross the border.

He allowed us to carry on, making us promise to turn left on to the link road at the white building. So what did we do when we got to white building?

'Polly, what are you doing?'

'I'm turning left like we were told to.' I have never been anything but law-abiding.

'We're not turning left.' Lee proclaimed.

'What do you mean we're not turning left? We were ordered to turn left.'

'No, we have to keep on going. Finn said nothing in his notes about turning left. We will never make it to Baghmara tonight if we leave this road.' Tim had sided with Lee.

'I really think we should turn left, the soldier obviously told us to turn left for a reason.'

'Do you believe everything you're told?'

'More often than not, yes I do.'

This actually isn't correct. I always believe everything I'm told. It is not something I am particularly proud of but I blame it on my ballet training and the threat of the stick. Long after my contemporaries had entered the sophisticated, sceptical phase I was still stuck, unquestioningly believing all that was said to me. Until I learnt a lesson the hard way.

Picture an effervescent night on a Greek island. A night when the moonlight bounces off ancient white walls, the click of high heels on cobbled streets being lured to the distant throb of music across the bay; a bar full of people clutching drinks all secretly amazed at the ease of entering witty conversation with strangers. The atmosphere is reckless, bacchanal and a million miles removed from the stringent codes of home. Enter a fellow countryman with a mellifluous voice that could melt a thousand ice cubes, the slickest, smoothest talker in town. Offer me a man with a broad chest or one with a broad vocabulary and I will pick the latter any day. He interrupts my flow of conversation.

'God! God you're lovely.'

Bowled over that this stranger has actually recognised my innate loveliness after only five minutes I carry on with extra confidence. He interrupts me again.

'No! You are seriously lovely. Why haven't we met before? I go home tomorrow. I can't believe it. I'll go home and you will forget you ever met me. You won't believe this but ever since I was little I wanted to marry a dancer. Did you say you dance? Please stay right here, I am going to find us some more alcohol. Say you'll at least spend these last few hours we have together?'

I awoke the next morning without so much as a note.

If, on the other hand, I had studied the 'Little Book of Bullshit' that other women seem to have degrees in, then I would have been able to interpret it thus:

'God! You're lovely.' (She'll be alright to add to my holiday list of conquests.)

'No! You're seriously lovely.' (Make the point a second time to make her believe that her loveliness evokes spontaneous outbursts that cannot be confined to the normal structure of chatting someone up.)

'Did you say you dance?' (Great! My very own lap dancer.)

'I go home tomorrow.' (Make her aware of the immediacy of the situation, can't be doing with coy flirting for the next week.)

'I am going to find us some more alcohol.' (Let's make sure that she's fully tanked-up.)

'Say you'll spend these last few hours we have together?' (Get her to commit to the rest of the night so as not to have to go in search of option number two.)

But I was not in a Greek bar now, I was inches from a potentially dangerous international border and I believed what I was told. It was the voice of authority speaking although some may say even more reason to take the information lightly. Tim and Lee were convinced that we should stay on the same road. If we came across more soldiers from the Border Security Force then we would tell them that their colleagues knew we were here, hoping that they would assume we had permission. In this way we were not telling lies, just refraining from telling the whole truth. The notes said it was a direct road to Baghmara, and a direct road is what we needed. I was not convinced that their reasoning would work and I let it be known in a battle-axe, huffing, puffing sort of way.

The smooth, straight road suddenly stopped to be replaced by a footpath. I could tell that Tim and Lee daren't look round at me. We juddered over stones, then dirt, then gravel, then grass then back to stones again. So this was the supposed Border Road that Finn travelled. I didn't think so, this road obviously wasn't, nor ever had been, tar-sealed. Everything on our bicycles was shaking, nuts and bolts rattled, pannier racks came unfastened. I was now spitting venom at Tim's back.

'Why do you guys refuse to listen to my opinion? Why are you

both so pigheaded? I knew he told us to turn left for a reason. Shit!
Where are we going to sleep tonight? We are in the middle of bloody
nowhere.'

'Polly, what do you want me to do about it? You want to turn
back? OK we'll turn back.' Tim's voice rose in exasperation.

'We can't turn back, we have wasted forty-five minutes of
daylight as it is, we'll never make it if we turn back.'

'Yep, you're right. We have to keep going, but we'll make it.
We still have two hours left before it gets dark.'

Inside my organs were doing funny things, I felt like Edvard
Munch's painting of *The Scream*.

Tim is a person without guile, an honourable and reassuring
quality that cannot be labelled to too many of us. He is one of the few
people who informs his life by primal instincts, rarely swayed by
conscious reasoning or indulging in hysteria. When you are on the
receiving end of this virtue, for I do believe it is an immeasurable virtue,
you cannot help yourself from feeling that you could take on the world.
If he were to look at you, with his wise, unfaltering eyes, it would seem
like your fears and insecurities were melting away. Everything would
seem bearable if this man were by your side. I always rely on Tim to
give it to me straight – he is what I call my bullshit barometer. But
with his last statement I had my suspicions that he was placating me.

It was inevitable. We were stopped a short while later by another
group of soldiers who sprung out of the woods they were patrolling.
We told our story in a rather offhand manner, explaining that we had
already been through all of these procedures, everything was fine but
time was pressing on, we really couldn't dally any longer. This time
there was a big problem with the language barrier, this group did not
speak a word of English between them and our Hindu consisted of one
word. Thankfully, a commuter on a bicycle was just passing our

Banana sellers - Meghalaya

Chicks with sticks!

What a commotion our bikes caused!

Dancing with the locals in the Saraswati festival, Darjeeling.

The Siddharta highway - I think I prefer my bike anyday!

Glenna, Tim and Lee and our police escorts on the way to the Orang
Sanctuary, Assam.

Tim fraternising with the locals on the road to Mangaldai, Assam.

Tim and I

frustrating scene. Don't ask me where he learnt his English but he gave up his immediate plans and became our translator.

'You must follow these men to the head camp.'

'But we can't,' we all cried. 'We don't have enough time.'

'Plenty of time! Please, follow.'

We were made to dismount and walk for several kilometres until we reached the camp. We felt like rebuked children caught trespassing. I still couldn't bring myself to talk civilly to Tim and Lee. We pushed our bikes in silence, heading inland away from the border. I was incapable of conjuring up any positive thoughts. I vehemently wanted to pour out my fear and anger on to the boys and yet I suspected that I had already gone too far. Both Tim and Lee were feeling exasperated but I would have been surprised if they were scared. Maybe it was a female thing and, if so, all the more reason to stomach my disquietude. I had chosen to come on this journey after all, this journey that was originally just for two blokes.

The guards and the translator took a left turning up a grassy path into a wood. There in the wooded enclave was the Indian equivalent of '*It Ain't 'Alf Hot Mum*': a number of bamboo huts, a volleyball net and numerous soldiers lolling about in varying degrees of undress. Our entrance caused a stir, soldiers appeared from all corners of the camp. We were ordered to sit on a bench. A chair was placed opposite us awaiting the chief of the outpost. We knew the situation was important, no tea was offered. The chief arrived and our passports were handed over and subsequently passed from soldier to soldier. Neither the chief nor any of the soldiers spoke English, so the procedures were conducted through the local villager. Once the excitement of our passports died down the men set about displaying their machismo, fawning and pawing each other, then entering into mock fights to show us how hard they were. Tired of that game they stalked around our bikes, prodding and poking until they came upon my Noddy bell. They pointed and giggled at it for about five minutes until the leader of the gang, a rifled, moustachioed hunk, finally did the noble deed of ringing it. They found this hilarious and utterly absorbing for a disturbing amount of time.

Meanwhile, in the background someone was winding up the radio transmitter. It crackled and spluttered across the camp. The operator bellowed into it - silence - then a barely audible response. He read out our details:

'HER NAME - MISS FARNHAM ROYAL.'

I beckoned the translator over. 'Please tell the operator that I was born in Farnham Royal, my name is Polly Benge.'

'SHE IS THIRTY-FOUR.'

I beckoned the translator over again. 'Please tell the operator that my house is number thirty-four, I am twenty-nine.'

If it wasn't for the fact that our onward journey was now doomed our interlude at the outpost would have been enormously entertaining. Instead, I looked at the fading sky and wondered for the hundredth time that afternoon where we were going to sleep that night.

When they finally accepted that they didn't know what else to do with us we were allowed to go. But, 'NO BORDER ROAD. JOIN LINK ROAD.'

'OK, that's fine. Thank you. Goodbye.'

Quick as a flash we were out of the camp dragging our invaluable translator with us. He guided us through more paths onto the link road. Our worst fears were confirmed, we had missed the last bus.

'Can we hitch?'

'I am thinking it is not possible. All trucks finished now.'

Oh no they hadn't. A solitary truck rumbled into view. It stopped and the driver and his co-pilot said they would take us to Baghmara. One would have been hard pushed to find a happier woman than I.

One would also have been hard pushed to find a man more aggrieved than Tim. In the cab there was only room for three, the driver, the co-driver and me. That was until Lee found out that the truck was in fact a coal truck. He was not going to endure the coal dust and keep Tim company if there was the merest, slimmest chance of fitting into the cab. Is this what they mean by an opportunist? For one and a half hours we all endured the most gut-wrenching, knuckle-whitening ride of our lifetimes.

The life of a truck driver is a hard one. They suffer inhumane hours, working for greedy bosses who pay little attention to safety regulations so long as maximum cargo is on board. The smallest of knocks can capsize a fully laden truck. Their wits are sharp but they are often stubborn, refusing to make way for an oncoming vehicle until it's too late. There is a dedicated allegiance between the driver and the assistant whose job it is to light their cigarettes, clean the windscreen, fetch their tea and keep them awake by the most effective technique possible. Our truck driver was mute, his only acknowledgement to his assistant was a curt nod every ten minutes to signal a new packet of *paan*. I kept wishing that the assistant, like a fussing wife, would tell him that he had consumed enough, but no chance, his addiction was acute.

I was so terrified that I hadn't taken a breath for about half an hour. He careered round blind bends with such unfailing confidence that I did find myself wondering if he possessed a sixth sense. I kept a running monologue in my head, re-assuring myself that he did this journey regularly. His use of the brakes was rare, preferring instead to negotiate the bridges and bends by turning the wheel in furious jabs: two with the right, three with the left, five with the right - our bodies whiplashing accordingly. I managed to crane my head to see how Tim was faring in the back, all I could see was a billowing T-shirt and neck tendons as thick and rigid as pylons.

Lee and I arrived in Baghmara shaken and white; Tim arrived in Baghmara livid and black. If we thought it was hairy inside the cab Tim had endured a far worse ordeal. He had to cling to the sides for the entire duration using all of his strength to keep himself and the bikes from being thrown around the truck.

The lines of communication had not reached this far, the town authorities had received no news of us. Too tired to worry we piled into the police station and filled in our details. This time we could deface their pristine ledgers with coal smudges.

They took us in convoy to the Forestry Inspection Bungalow where they managed to find a room for us. It was basic with two buckets of cold water and two narrow single beds between us. We had to eke out the water. Tim was black from head to toe; he insisted he had the biggest share.

There was no food for us at the Inspection Bungalow and the deputy was mortified that his domain could not offer more amenities. He called for his men to drive us into town to the only place that was still serving food. It was 8.00 pm. We drove through the ghostly streets and over a wide, still river. Barely a soul was out and apart from the few kerosene lanterns and the glow from the stars, the town was dark and quiet. We had been warned that Baghmara is another headquarters of the Garo militants and people should avoid going out after dark, especially us.

The Fooding Inn was gloomy and filthy with no welcoming ambience to speak of. After the day we had had an Italian trattoria, with clean checked tablecloths and a candle in a raffia-covered bottle, would have gone down a treat. Instead, a man shuffled over to our bench with a couple of saucepans and congealed ladles. He dollopped the food on to stainless steel platters and poured us some grey water from a plastic jug. We wolfed down our rice, not wishing to linger in the desperate atmosphere or indeed in our hostile moods. We had eaten breakfast, lunch and dinner together for one month now; tonight there was absolutely nothing I could think of to say to them.

Back at the Inspection Bungalow the deputy came into our room for a chat. Something had happened to him in the hour we had been away, he appeared to be one pancake short of a stack. As the alcohol fumes billowed out, we got our answer - he was absolutely plastered. Baghmara, it seemed, was the hardship post for the employees of the Forestry Department. There was nothing in this bleak town that could come anywhere near the term recreational except for alcohol. But even then there were no bars to sit in to blot out the loneliness of this posting. After their work for the day was over it was back to the four peeling walls of their rooms and the comfort of the glass bottle in their hand.

It was very apparent that he wanted to stay and chat. The prospect might have seemed more enticing if he had brought his bottle of moonshine in with him. We hadn't had a drop of alcohol since our gin and tonics up in Darjeeling and I am not ashamed to say that I was gagging. We sat with him for a while until I felt like it should be me to make the first movements towards going to bed. He took the hint and stumbled to his own quarters across the veranda.

A subtle change had taken place in us that day; resentments had been born. Where once we were a unit, now we were single entities. In opting to travel in the cab of the truck, instead of helping in the back, Tim had lost some respect for Lee. One small action and yet it dented the regard in which he held him. Is the esteem we hold for people really that precarious? Yes. It is a different issue to liking and disliking, forgiving and understanding. Those feelings seem to ebb and flow capriciously, but respect for another can be extinguished almost instantly like a light bulb that suddenly dies; one word, one sentence, one action

– POW – gone. In times such as these kinship is vital; it is the difference between turning the trials of travel into fulfilling conquests or into exhausting battles. For Tim, his comrade in arms had let him down, Lee would have to regain his respect. From now on each action would be subconsciously assessed.

We sat around the table by candlelight, eating a cake we had bought in Tura that morning and playing a listless game of dice, consumed with our own thoughts. I was still quietly simmering that my opinion back at the turning had been so blatantly disregarded. I was angry with myself for not having more strength of my convictions.

Lee climbed into his sleeping bag and tuned into the World Service on his headphones. He must have been missing Glenna, poor sod. I hoped that there was football on the radio to provide some vestige of comfort. You could never meet a more dedicated Coventry supporter than Lee. Every Saturday night since the trip began Lee had listened to a live match on the radio; one Saturday in Nepal he lucked out, it was a home match for Coventry.

I was always the last into bed, oh to have the skin-care nonchalance of a man. I tried to adhere to some kind of a beauty routine but my discipline and essential materials were often lacking. Apart from the paternal attempts by Tim and Lee to clean me up before meeting people, I revelled in not giving a damn about my appearance.

I got under the mosquito net and searched for holes. There were only a couple but with a bit of careful arrangement I could get away with not having to get out my needle and cotton. I told Tim that on no account could he move around in his sleep otherwise we would end up a feast for some lucky mosquito. There was no room anyway, we stuck ourselves together in the impossibly narrow bed. As he drew me towards him I felt all my animosity flow away. God I loved him. New Zealand? New Zealand! New Zealand - my head rung with the name. What would I do there? Would I like it? Is he really serious about wanting me with him? Every time he breathed in I felt his stomach expand to fill the small of my back. To bear witness to another's life and breath in such intimacy must surely be the most important thing we could do with our lives and in succumbing to real love forget ourselves utterly and entirely.

Tonight was not the night to battle out my decision. Mothers are right, issues at night loom larger then they do during the day. And anyway, I still had eighteen more sleeps with him to go.

"In the spice shop she crushed leaves of sage and oregano in the palms of her hands for the pure pleasure of smelling them, and brought a handful of cloves, another star of anise, and one each of ginger root and juniper, and she walked away with tears of laughter in her eyes because the smell of cayenne pepper made her sneeze so much."

Gabriel Garcia Marquez

11
THE MINDREADING CHOWDIKKAR

We were heading for the game reserve of Balpakram, a national wildlife park high up on a plateau, known to the locals as "abode of perpetual winds". Some also believe it is here that the spirits of the dead dwell before embarking on the final journey. It is also home to tigers, elephants, carnivorous plants and the most ancient, sacred trees in India.

The notes told us (my confidence in them was lessening) to allow eight hours cycling to get up there. Once at the plateau we would find nothing save for the Forestry Inspection Bungalow and, although there would be chowdikkars to look after us, we had to take all of our provisions with us. By the time we arrived last night it was too late to go and buy anything and if we were to cycle it meant leaving at 6.00 am. We could not delay a day, so we had no choice but to take the bus.

Baghmara looked a little more lively in the morning, the usual market hustle and bustle was in full swing. Where did these people disappear to come nightfall? We went to buy our food trying not to invite much attention; who was to say our vegetable seller wasn't a violent militant in disguise? Sure enough we were interrupted by two tall gentlemen who stuck out from the rest of the locals. They asked to see our details; Lee started to vent his wrath but one of the men stopped him.

'Please, not to be getting angry sir. We are undercover policemen, we are just to be checking that everything is alright.'

Chastised, we thanked them. This town had more to offer than others of its ilk, namely spirits. The palliative liquid was sold in kiosks behind impenetrable bars. Seeing these bars immediately took me back to my first few years in the Northern Ballet Theatre. The headquarters for the NBT were smack in the middle of a council estate in Manchester called Hulme. Hulme was notorious for a number of reasons. When it was built in the fifties it was not only the largest council estate in Europe but it was also built of asbestos. By the middle of the eighties medical research had shown that asbestos was highly toxic and was seriously damaging people's health. The residents of Hulme were relocated leaving building upon building of derelict flats. Enter the drug dealers, the drug addicts, society's dropouts, thieves and muggers, the homeless and Mad Mary.

Turning left into the estate from Moss Side the first thing the visitor was greeted with was virulent graffiti, 'WE ARE POOR AND ANGRY' and other vehement testaments to a discontented ghetto. Each brick, each blade of grass, each cloud that perpetually hung over Hulme was imbued with a sense of apathy and defeatism. There were two pubs on the estate, the sort of buildings where one might think the council planners hadn't been able to decide whether to have a loo block or a pub.

Once inside, if one dared to enter, the bar was difficult to locate through the thick clouds of Regal cigarette smoke. They served Boddingtons and orange or peach 20/20 – fortified wine, and not a lot else. The women strove to look glamorous, but no amount of hair dye or pearlised nail varnish could disguise the bar code of lines on the top lip, from decades of chain-smoking, or the unhealthy pallor. The men's moustaches had a yellow tinge from nicotine, their faces sported a couple of scars and watery, pale eyes. One drink was enough to make one vow never to return.

The shops in the small precinct were basic and perfunctory. The small supermarket sold only Happy Shopper brand goods and a variety of meat and potato pies; if you wanted cheese it was packets of processed or nothing. The chippie did a roaring trade, not so much in the fish but in chip butties or battered savaloy. There was a small chemist selling variations of pearlised nail varnish and an off-license, the bottles of liquor an unattainable mirage unless the morose man deigned to serve you.

In the middle of this bleak cityscape was a listed building, Zion House. If buildings were to have the equivalent of body doubles then it could have been cast as the house in the Adam's Family. If one was feeling generous you could call it handsome, if not then a gothic eyesore. It was home to the Northern Ballet Theatre and the Hallé Orchestra on a Thursday night.

In empty flats people were shooting-up to the strains of Tchaikovsky being thumped out on the rehearsal piano. The incongruous pitter-patter of twenty pairs of pointe shoes drowned out the cries of people being stabbed outside the offie. In our lunch hour we tripped down to the shops to buy a raspberry yoghurt and twenty Silk Cut dressed unconcernedly in leotards and tights.

They never harmed us, only our cars. At least four times a week one of our cars was broken into. The Musicians Union demanded a guard when the Hallé came to rehearse; Equity didn't, our No Claims bonus points were a thing of the past. We didn't put up much of a fight for one either, we were too busy trying to perfect our *petit battement* to mastermind a strike on behalf of our car stereos.

It was a grim place but it did not seem to quell our artistic enterprises, creativity shall conquer no matter the location. Besides, we had our caretaker Michael, a broad Ulster man, to amuse us throughout the day. We ordered three cups of tea, even if we only wanted two, just to hear him say, 'That'll be dirty pants please.'

The estate no longer exists but Zion House remains intact, standing alone in the wasteland of Hulme. Give the place a couple of years and no doubt it will be described as 'the up and coming' area of

Manchester. The Northern Ballet Theatre left a long time ago. I think the Hallé still rehearse there but one job will have been lost; they no longer have need for a guard.

The bus had now arrived in the square and there was a fever of activity. The boys hoiked our poor cycles up on to the roof along with chairs and wicker baskets, sacks of rice and a dozen people. We tried to ascertain how long the journey would take us but as usual we were left none the wiser, some said two hours, others said five. Why worry? We would get there eventually. To our dismay every seat was taken in the bus. Now the e.t.a. was a little more crucial. However the locals thought it inconceivable that we should we have to stand. Without any prompting they set about organising everybody in the bus so that the three of us had seats.

Do not for a moment envisage City Hopper seats or Double Decker seats that we are spoilt with at home; these seats were a wooden bench with a padded back and exploding innards spewing out in all directions rather like Mr Creosote in Monty Python. Each seat supposedly held three people but only if they were afflicted with some wasting disease. The plus points were our own foot ventilation provided by two chickens who when became nervous, which was nearly all the time, flapped their wings excitably causing a very pleasing breeze. They seemed to find Tim's ankles quite tasty and were not shy about having a little nip at them every so often.

Hours passed as we made our way up to the plateau of Balpakram. We climbed up through thick jungle as the plains of Bangladesh swept away into the horizon on our right. The villages became less frequent. We would drive for an hour then stop at what seemed to be just a grassy path leading into the jungle. Activity on the roof commenced and a huddle of people would get off, balancing the chairs on their heads and sacks of rice on their hips and disappear off into the trees. I pictured the shack with the new pair of chairs placed like thrones in the quintessence of minimalist living.

It is funny how quickly hours pass when one is removed from a habitual routine. If I had to go to Edinburgh by coach, despite the luxuries of videos and refreshment trolleys, I would beg, borrow and steal to go by train, but even a train would push my levels of endurance. I would try desperately hard to go by sleeper and, if that were not an option, then I would contemplate forking out for a plane ticket. But on this trip I was enduring unfathomable hours of travel in vehicles that you would not put your pet hamster in back at home. On the contrary, I looked forward to these journeys mainly because it meant I wasn't on the saddle and I loved the opportunity to day-dream the hours away, wallowing in idle thought as my eyes scanned the distance into alien territory. When bored of conversing with myself I had only to turn my head and look at my fellow passengers to entertain myself for another hour.

In amongst a crowd I found that there was always one face of indescribable beauty. The beauty was sometimes the contour of a head, or the slope of a forehead or the arch of an eyebrow that made me stare unashamedly.

I adopted another game to while away the hours. It was more of a test to see how my squeamishness had evolved. Just as there was always someone beautiful, there was always someone that nature had been unkind to. Until last week I would have immediately turned my head from any abnormality, seeking refuge in staring at my hands hoping that by not looking I could pretend that it didn't exist. This game entailed looking at these abnormalities, really looking at them and withstanding the desire to quickly avert my eyes. Of course my scrutiny had to be subtle which was somewhat of a problem as every person in the bus, blessed or afflicted, stared at us unflinchingly for the entire duration of the trip. In the end I thought that if they could stare so blatantly at us, then we could do likewise to them.

On this particular bus I carried out my test on a man sitting on a sack of rice in the aisle - he had no toenails. Where the toenails should have been was rough and blackened skin so that the man's toes ended in engorged, gnarly stumps splaying over the rims of his flip-flops. Others had rogue eyes, skin diseases or one tooth. Old women lifted their arms showing midriffs wrinkled and leathered from the years of sun, collagen a distant memory.

I think we are all body-snoopers on the quiet. I know that perhaps I am more body conscious than most but I would prefer to view a live exhibition of naked bodies than an exhibition of Cubist art any day. I promise I could look you in the eye and say that this is not a confession from a voyeuristic pervert, more someone with an insatiable curiosity for the marvels of the human form. Moles and birthmarks, long narrow legs, thick ankles, calve muscles that swell more on the outside of the shin than on the inside, the fifth vertebra of the cervical spine that sticks out rather than running flush with the rest of the vertebral column, shoulders that are broad, shoulder blades that are flat, gaps at the top of thighs, gaps between the teeth, scars and veins, perfections and imperfections - I am fascinated by them all.

These observations then progress into wondering how the owners of these features feel towards their particular uniqueness. How much time do people waste worrying about their beaky nose for instance? Do they look at a retroussé nose and think how their life would be different if they owned a nose like that? What about a woman with flawless legs? Does she relish summer coming so that she can show them off in skimpy skirts and careless abandon? Ask a woman that question and I doubt you would get a truthful reply - of course not, it would shriek narcissism. But who wouldn't enjoy preening and adorning if they were the owners of such an aesthetic accoutrement? She is oblivious that for some women summer means curling their legs underneath them to hide the freckles and the whiteness, the splotches and the cellulite, the heat and the glare of the sun reminding them that they are in possession of something far from perfect.

I was born with (or at least soon developed) a bright red spot, rather like a mole, just underneath the bottom lashes on my left eye. It is a physical flaw that I think about perhaps three times a year. It is only when a young child points at my red spot with wide eyes and says 'hurt, hurt' that I worry that maybe it is unsightly and that adults are just too polite to say anything. It never occurs to me to do anything about it, although one friend did helpfully say, 'Make it a feature darling, tattoo it!'

But take the small patch of broken veins on my anklebone and I will alarm you with the strength of my feelings that I pour into this delta of imperfection. One would have to be kissing my ankle to notice them and yet, if I was even moderately well-off, they would be the first things to go in my visits to the beauty shop. It is wear and tear together with self-abuse that depresses us about our imperfections. I can blame the gap between my front teeth on Grandpa Churcher, but for my receding gums I can only berate myself. I should have given up smoking sooner, I should have listened to my dentist when she told me I had to floss.

I remember a story I was told about a certain princess who at the age of sixty did not have one wrinkle on her face. She was famed throughout…? (I can't remember where, the nature of the story was too intriguing to retain geographical information) for her perfect skin. Her secret was that at a ridiculously young age she made a vow to herself not to ever show any expression on her face whatsoever. She didn't smile, she didn't frown, she even yawned keeping her mouth shut and she didn't go outside. Whilst ninety-eight percent of our reasoning thinks stupid bloody cow, the other two percent makes a mental note to tone down the Gurna-type grimacing that comes to us so readily.

Five hours later the bus creaked round a corner and stopped. Everyone looked at us.

'Why are we stopping?'

'Balpakram! Balpakram!'

'But we're in the middle of nowhere.'

'Yes! Balpakram.'

We scrabbled around for our belongings and got the bikes down from the roof. The bus continued on its way leaving us standing in the middle of the road feeling small and bewildered. I didn't know what I was expecting, perhaps an Abercrombie and Kent jeep to whizz past us full of khaki-clad game spotters returning to luxury tents after a day of tiger-spotting. But there was nothing.

We noticed a track with some scant buildings at the end. We cycled up. Everywhere was deathly quiet apart from a voracious dog that came snapping at our heels. One by one men appeared out of the doorways of the buildings and lent on the doorframes regarding us coolly.

'Inspection Bungalow?'

A guy smoking a cigarette nodded to the house at the end of the drive. We offered a smile but none was returned. We reached the house and another man came out. He had a couple of badges on his uniform so we took him to be someone of importance and gave him our letter of introduction. We had just assumed it would be all right but the seriousness of our dependency on these people suddenly sank in and I felt myself go hot and cold all over. He listed a string of problems.

'No food, no water - we expecting you but the boss has not been for long time. He supposed to come and pay our wages but he not come.'

No wonder they all looked pissed off, an absent boss on pay-day is not a reason to look cheerful. Their money was one week late. The deputy called over a sub-deputy to take us to our accommodation.

We walked back onto the road for a little while and then took a path leading into the jungle. Eventually we arrived at a gracious building painted soft yellow set amongst palm trees and pampas grasses. The house and grounds were perched on an apron of land with views over two hundred and forty square feet of National Park jungle. It was awesome. The house had a colonial air although it wasn't that old. It had a meshed veranda with comfy floral armchairs and side-tables, a bizarre horseshoe conference table in the dining room and three large bedrooms. The kitchen was outside with open fires with huge pots of water simmering on the top. There was no electricity or running water and the nearest village was miles away. I felt I was in the remotest place I had ever been. I could not even begin to guess where the nearest hospital was. I just had to hope I would get used to it.

We had two chowdikkars to look after us which they did willingly if not that efficiently. We gathered that their services were not called for that often. Tim took over and made us a huge stir-fry over the open fire in the kitchen, the woodsmoke smarting our eyes so that we had to watch over the noodles in shifts. When it became dark we ate and wrote our diaries by lanterns. I sat on one of the chairs on the veranda, my ears buzzing with the sound of silence, every now and then hearing an elephant cry far off in the distance.

The boys seemed perfectly at ease with the remoteness; I was all a quiver, startling at any strange sound and blocking from my mind the miles and miles of jungle and plains that separated us from civilisation. Had I really become that urbanised? When the lanterns were running low we had to go to bed. The chowdikkars came to lock us in. Why? An easy target for needy militants or to ward off dexterous tigers, I didn't know. Tim fell asleep instantly while I tossed and turned, my ears straining for untoward sounds. At one point I heard men's voices outside our window and then someone rattling the door. I shook Tim awake and we sat together under the mosquito net every sense vibrating with concentration. Whoever it was went away and eventually I fell asleep.

I awoke in the morning feeling like a million dollars. I had slept a night in this place, it was time to do away with my phobia and enjoy the spectacular beauty of it all. It was still early in the morning as I walked to the lip of the apron to stare out into the jungle. There were sounds and activity everywhere. I stood for a while watching a family of monkeys make their way across the roof of the jungle performing death defying dives, at each tree stopping for a snack and a gossip. I still couldn't believe where I was.

Back in the kitchen the boys were discussing the food for the day with the chowdikkars. In our rush to get off the bus we had left a bag of food behind and we needed some more. Knowing how far it was to the village we let one of them go on my bike; he was tickled pink thinking of the reaction he would receive from his mates when he rolled into the market on my Dawes Horizon. Three hours later he returned by which time we were thinking that maybe he had done a runner or that each person in the village wanted a ride on the bike. He had managed to get most things on the list plus orange squash, chocolate biscuits and a packet of tea - funnily enough the exact items we had left on the bus! We had given him a ridiculous amount of money and when we asked for the change he shook his head vehemently.

'No changing, all money on these (pointing to our abandoned groceries). I am thinking you are liking these.'

Hah, he was a clever knickers!

'No! These are the things we left on the bus yesterday, we have already paid for them.'

Suddenly, his understanding of the English language evaded him.

We spent the morning lolling around the house and gardens. Lee was very weak; he is a slight man anyway but now he was looking on the skeletal side. Tim and I went to see the deputy hoping to go game spotting and left Lee behind to rest. The officer had still not showed up with their wages which meant, as far as we were concerned, there was no jeep to take us into the park. I was disappointed. Instead, the deputy enlisted us into the care of a warden and off we went on a walk.

We followed a path into the jungle stepping over ridges and troughs made by the elephants. The most exquisite butterflies flew across our path. It was hot and airless. We walked for an hour in silence following our warden with his rifle slung over his shoulder. Eventually he stopped at a clearing and beckoned us over. Below us for as far as the eye could see was jungle, one uninterrupted carpet of tree tops. To the right of us the carpet swept upwards onto the plateau. This was where the real animal action took place. The only way to get there was by jeep, this was as far as our walk would take us. We turned on our heels and retraced our steps back to the camp.

It was my guess that not a great deal of talking goes on in these parts; the veranda was littered with khaki-clad wardens but no one was speaking. We even sat for a while and still no one spoke. I suppose there is not really a lot to say, the days don't differ that much. The elephants may have moved from one corner of the park over to the other leaving a trail of cannonball elephant dung in their wake. But once that has been discussed where does the conversation progress from there? After a while we got up and ambled home. The silence was infectious.

I was not looking forward to going back to the house, for some reason that day I was feeling quarrelsome and stifled. It dawned on me that never had I laughed so little as in these past weeks. Even during a bleak period in my life when work seemed to evade me, I still managed to find some pathetic humour in it all. Shortly after I left the NBT and returned to London I signed on with a few dance agencies. Their part of the deal was to send me along to all manner of auditions as a five foot eight blonde. My job was to re-invent myself as anything from a Bond girl for a charity gala to a dancing stick of celery for a Hellmann's Mayonnaise commercial. Unfortunately, there were often other five foot eight blondes who were that little bit stringier than me or looked more vampish in black dresses. Losing all sense of perspective when it came to evaluating my talent, I often came home seeking sympathy from my flatmates.

'I don't understand why I didn't get chosen. Look at me! I'm perfect to be a stick of celery.'

'Could you perhaps have tried for the cucumber role?' Geoff said helpfully - hopefully.

'No, the cucumbers had already been cast. God, Geoff what's wrong with me?'

'Nothing is wrong with you. Perhaps your skin tone wasn't right. Take it as a compliment.'

'Yeah thanks! Anyway how was your day?'

'Really interesting, I interviewed an astronomer at NASA about the comet.'

'That's great, that's ...er... an interesting day.'

Geoff had a worthwhile job as a science producer for the BBC World Service; I couldn't even get a job as a bloody crudité.

There was silence.

'What about the carrots?'

'Not a hope in hell, there was a posse of redheads there.'

We ended up laughing a lot.

One of the worst days in my life involved singing. I cannot nor ever will be able to sing. This particular audition was for *Copa Cabana*, the new musical by Barry Manilow based around the story of Lola and the immortalised nightclub. I breezed through the first round of auditions. God was on my side – the singing was in groups. I was recalled a few days later, my lip-syncing had paid off. This time the auditions were held in a West End theatre and His Royal Barryness was there to pick the cast himself. We were split into groups and told that the dancing part would come first. Right, I said to myself, this is where I make my mark. I inched my way to the front of the stage, leaping and spinning with the commitment of a thoroughbred racehorse. I felt good, I felt in control. Others were getting chucked out in their droves as we performed the sequence over and over again, with each repetition I felt myself embodying the style they wanted. The first whittling down of people was now over, it was time for the singing.

'Let it be group singing. Let it be group singing.' I repeated to myself like a mantra.

The bigger breasted girls who were obviously in this business for their voices suddenly came to life launching into a chorus of scales. I attempted a few tentative scales of my own and then swiftly shut-up; just as I had thought, the voice fairy had not come to me in the night. The pianist sat himself down and we gathered around the baby grand. Just as the pianist was placing his hands on the keys Barry leapt onto the stage shooing the accompanist away and seating himself on the piano stool. This was the cue needed for a barrage of photographers and journalists to gather round the piano clicking and flashing in a frenzy of Barrymania.

'OK! Let's here you girls sing.' Famous fingers started tapping out the first lines of one of the most famous songs in history, 'Her name was Lola, she was a showgirl ....'

CLICK, CLICK, FLASH, CLICK.FLASH, FLASH, FLASH.

Here was someone who knew how to milk a photo opportunity. We sang through the verse a couple of times, twelve girls, Barry and me. It all had a cosy, chummy feel to it and despite my shaky legs I was beginning to enjoy myself. Until…

'OK, let's have it from the top one by one.'

I stopped breathing. I looked around for my escape route. Perhaps I could just edge towards the wings and make a quick dash for it. Or I could drop to my knees on the pretence of adjusting my leg warmer then crawl through the piano legs into the auditorium and out onto the Strand. It was now or never. The first girl started singing and I froze, never in my life had I heard such a fantastic voice at close quarters. Barry looked impressed too. The second girl started and the hairs on my arms shot up vertically, she had the voice of a real showgirl. The third and then the fourth sang the verse, each as good as the last. Barry, shaking his immaculate head of hair, was visibly overwhelmed.

'Wow! You girls can really sing.'

I was number thirteen, as if I needed that inauspicious number to add to my mounting terror. Come number eleven I began to shake, twelve and I thought I was going to be sick. It eventually happened that one of the most famous noses in showbiz history was staring up at me, eyes that women travel all over the world to catch a glimpse of, looking at me expectantly, cameras pointing from every direction. I started.

'Her name was…Lola…she was a showgirl. She had … da da da in her hair (my vision was beginning to swim…what the f... did she have in her hair?) and music all around…everywhere. Music and fass...passion was always the pass...fashion, at the Copa...they fell…'

I was jumping from key to key with the speed of a trampolinist, my voice getting weedier and weedier. GOD SOMEONE HELP ME OUT PLEASE. I was willing Barry to come to my rescue and put me out of my misery. It was obvious I was making a fool out of myself and it was torture for everyone else too. I noticed them all staring at the floor, probably thinking if they were to make eye contact with anyone else they would lose all self-control. The cameras had stopped clicking and the journalists were busy looking down at their notes. I took one last deep breath:

'They fell in love.'

I didn't get that job either.

We were nearing the bungalow and my mood hadn't lifted. This was the first day that we didn't have to go somewhere or organise something since we were in Pokhara. The afternoon lay ahead with nothing to do but relax. Yet that was the thing I felt least able to do. We got back to the bungalow and said hello to Lee who was still sitting on the veranda where we had left him. It wasn't just me, we were all feeling irritable and listless, the adventure of travel seemed to have lost some of its allure and all we wanted was a slice of home. The day reminded me of the odd days in the school holidays when you knew you should be having a good time yet none of your normal pastimes seemed to create much enthusiasm. This was when mothers - or at least my mother - would manage to conjure up some project to snap me out of my inertia. I looked at Tim, mmm - perhaps I would give him the Mother Test. I told him the story and adopted a challenging expression.

'OK! Give me an hour,' he said.

I went in search of spare water to do some washing; the chowdikkars let me have two buckets. Our clothes were black, every fibre ingrained with dirt. Two buckets weren't enough but the intention was there. I rigged up a line between two palm trees with some string that we carried with us. I hummed to myself. I had a feeling that I was being watched, whether by the big brown eyes of a local lad or by the eyes of a monkey, I wasn't sure. I was certain, however, that white M&S knickers were an intriguing sight in these parts.

Feeling hungry I went into the kitchen to make an omelette. The chowdikkars were sitting outside on stools talking softly, a woman was with them holding a small baby.

'Is it alright if I cook some food?'

They sprang up looking guilty at being found doing nothing. I was quite happy to potter by myself but they hovered around me eager to be helpful. I told them I was going to make an omelette, they looked at me uncomprehendingly. 'OK, I teach you a popular western dish.'

They handed me a knife with a rusty curved blade and a wooden handle and a block of wood stained yellow from years of turmeric and chilli. I delegated jobs; one chopped tomatoes, the other garlic, I cut the onion. The woman with the baby balanced it on her hip and stared at me from the corner of the kitchen. If only I knew what she was thinking. I would not have been surprised if perhaps she thought me grotesque. There was something about these tribal women that made me feel unfeminine and gauche. My short blonde hair seemed unsophisticated compared to her long sleek mane, her tatty sari complementing the curves of a woman much more becomingly than my shorts and expanse of pink flesh.

I beat the eggs in an old tin can and added the rest of the ingredients. There was a pan for boiling the drinking water, a pan for boiling the rice, a pan for the *dhal* and a deep wok for the curry. For them there was no menu change, each meal, day in day out, always the same. The wok had two handles and a stick running through the both of them so that it could be lifted on and off the fire with no need for cloths. It was staggeringly heavy. One of them stoked the fire underneath and I poured in the eggs. In an instant the little dingy room was filled with smoke and my eyes ran with tears. The men laughed, the woman stared. Once it was cooked I put some on a plate and took it over to her. She gave me her baby to hold, her nose crinkled up and she giggled as she put the first forkful in her mouth.

'Do you like it?'

She giggled again and nodded her head imperceptibly.

The hour was up and I went in search of Tim. I found him under the shade of a tree at the back of the house sawing at a long piece of bamboo. My restless mood had disappeared in the last hour, I felt in balance with the pace of the afternoon and I was happy to sit on the veranda and do nothing but stare out into the jungle. Tim's eyes were glowing with accomplishment and he ordered me inside to await his surprise. A few minutes later he came through the door carrying his present to me, it was a backgammon set. The board he had drawn onto the back of my diary and the pieces were cut from bamboo and coloured in with ink. It was enchanting. He enchanted me. I felt the luckiest woman alive.

"Crisis needs no rehearsal"

Oscar Wilde

12
HOSTAGES

It was early in the morning when we left the house. The "abode of perpetual winds" was perfectly still. I wondered why it was given that name, I had felt only the merest whisper of a breeze in the time I was there. I liked to think it alluded to the souls of the dead. A soul untethered from the confines of a body, relishing its freedom and whistling past the trees in a joyous dance of the departed.

Tomorrow night we would be in Shillong, we were on the last leg of our journey around Meghalaya. By tomorrow night we had to be in Shillong if we were to be in time to meet Glenna in Guwahati the following day. The notes for the day seemed straight forward:

"At Maheskola turn right on to border road until reaching river. Last boat across leaves 4.15pm. 15 k's to Ranikor. Circuit house."

This time the words 'border road' didn't faze me. We had now been questioned so many times that the authorities knew who we were and what we were doing. Besides there was no other road to Ranikor.

A day of staying in one place had done us all the world of good. Our legs felt charged once more and we were ready to burn up the kilometres to Ranikor. Our mood was light and carefree, the thought of returning to civilisation had mollified our temperaments and we felt a united band of travellers once more. Our conversation was of what lay ahead, hot showers, beer, porridge for breakfast and cakes. The habit of creature comforts so easy to recall yet so hard to forget.

The day was turning out to be a scorcher, the sun beat down on our backs as we tried to make steady progress. Past monsoons had made the road surface precarious for anything other than by foot. It wound up and down through the jungle rewarding our ascents with giddying views of wild treetops surrendering to the flood plains of Bangladesh.

We descended into Maheskola, a sleepy village straddling a river that fed the swampy pastures of the lowlands. We were starving and went in search of some breakfast. Perched on bamboo benches in a little shack we ate a bowl of smoky curry and drank sweet milky tea out of metal tumblers. Tea always came in tumblers, either glass or metal, but never in cups. We did wonders for the popularity of the chosen eatery. We had started to time it; on average it took five minutes for word to get round the village of our presence. In that short amount of time no bench was left empty and each window and doorway was filled with jostling faces. The audience inside the shack were the more affluent of the community, they could afford to 'eat out' enjoying the ringside seats.

An oldish man on my right tapped me on the arm, his nails seemingly too large for his fingers.

'You are eating *Sattva*,' he said in faltering English.

'*Sattva*? Is that the name of the dish? It tastes very good.'

'No. *Sattva* not name, *Sattva* is *guna*.'

I looked at Tim to see if he was following the threads of conversation better than me. By the shrug he gave me I guessed not. The man continued to explain. Hindus believe that all food substances fit into three *gunas* or qualities as once described in the *Bhagavad Gita*. *Sattva* is the highest quality for it promotes good health and also happiness. To enhance *Sattva* one must eat grains and pulses, vegetables and milk products. *Rajas* is the second and comes in rich or over-spiced foods. They consider this unhealthy for the food arouses passions which subsequently lead to disease.

The third is *Tamas*, food that is not fresh and therefore unclean. To eat *tamasic* food is not only unhealthy but they believe it leads to dullness and sloth, ignorance and decay until, finally, destruction. To many Hindus meat is considered *tamasic* for it is not in accordance with *Ahimsa*, non-violence or reverence for all life. It not only involves not causing physical harm but is a mental attitude in harmony with the moral codes of Hinduism. Mahatma Gandhi preached *Ahimsa*:

> *"Non-violence is not a garment to be put on and off at will. Its seat is in the heart, and it must be an inseparable part of our being."*

There are also a large proportion of Hindus who eat meat, refraining only from eating beef. I later found out that McDonalds had opened a restaurant in Delhi. Who were they expecting to eat there if not a large number of Hindus? They are not selling Big Macs but instead have invented the 'Maharaja Mac' made from mutton and a deep-fried vegetable patty! Taste and hygiene aside I would be sceptical of the term 'fast food'.

I pictured the scene; a counter of white-hatted clerks, the computerised tills replaced by ledgers, your order written down in perfect handwriting, 'Please to be serving you with one Maharaja Meal with the addition of 75ml of Coca-Cola and a siding order of tomato ketchup.'

At the end of the order the two-star McClerk would ask, 'Please to be putting your name and address here.' Your order would be put into a manila file and taken by a one-star McClerk into the kitchen. No thanks, give me a fresh *samosa* from the street vendor any day.

Now that we had fed ourselves on good *Sattva* we thought it time we embarked on the border road. We filled up our water bottles and said goodbye. A throng of people followed us to the turning, stopping as if at an invisible line.

'Ranikor?' we asked, pointing down a black, smooth tar-sealed road.

They nodded and waved us goodbye. I felt like I was in the

Wizard of Oz, saying goodbye to the munchkins and stepping onto the yellow-brick road with my ruby slippers, Tim as Scarecrow and Lee as Tin Man.

Ah, the blessed relief of riding on that surface. My bike felt transformed into an oiled racing car, I hardly had to do anything. We sped along effortlessly. The road weaved through the rusty wire fence much the same as a few days before but today there were no suspicious figures lurking behind the trees. All seemed tranquil on the border road.

We spoke too soon, ten minutes later a group of soldiers came into view. As we neared they stood up and blocked the way. We thought we would try a different approach this time, we would take control of the situation.

'Hello, hello, *Namaste,*' we chorused, our faces wreathed in smiles.

'You will need these,' we said officially and handed them our passports, opening them at the appropriate page to keep confusion to a minimum. We didn't allow them a second to doubt our intentions and immediately carried on to explain our route and to tell them we had permission. As an afterthought we got out a packet of cigarettes and offered them round. That turned out to be our winning move, one by one they lit up then clapped us on the back.

'We are sorry to be delaying you, please continue.'

And we shook hands.

Jubilant at our success we entertained no misgivings as to our onward journey. It was still only 11.00 am, it was forty-five kilometres to the river and then just a short distance to Ranikor. Time, for once, was on our hands and we could afford to take it leisurely.

The sun was shining in a cloudless sky, the road ahead lay smooth and enticing. This was going to be a great ride. If someone had asked me at that moment how I felt I doubt I could have found the words to express myself. I could have said I felt liberated, unshackled, full of optimism, resilient. I could have said I felt more alive than I had ever felt. And all would have been true, yet those words seemed to speak of a polarisation between positive and negative.

Liberation means a release from encumbrance, implying that to be burdened is a negative state. Life is full of burdens. It is only when we think of them as weights to be lifted on and off our shoulders that we bounce so erratically between good moods and bad. Likewise with optimism, if we weren't optimistic did it mean we were without hope? Is it not possible to just be? Neither optimistic for the future nor nostalgic for the past?

I was in the car with a friend one day, it was a wet Sunday afternoon in February and we were driving down country lanes. Every leaf on every branch was drooping, having given up on resisting the weight of the raindrops that had been relentlessly battering them all weekend. It was a gloomy scene without doubt. Out of the blue Sid said, 'I think I'm entering a melancholic phase. I get them sometimes.'

Looking out of the window I could sympathise and I went to put a comforting arm around his shoulder. My hand stopped before reaching its destination, so taken aback was I by his next sentence.

'Not that I mind, in fact in a perverse sort of way I quite enjoy being melancholic. Makes a change though doesn't it? It doesn't usually last for long, something always snaps me out of it.'

He was dead right. We so dread feeling angry, worse still depressed, anxious or jealous that in the very dreading we seem to invite them into our lives on a more routine basis. So abhorrent do we perceive these emotions to be that in the desire to be rid of them they seem to linger long past their shelf life. If we just managed to switch our mental attitude into accepting that we will experience these undesirable emotions, but just as long as we don't indulge or fixate upon them, then of course they will pass. It is like having the neighbour's cat come into your house. The more you chase it out, like quicksilver it slinks into the most inaccessible corner and stays put no matter how much coaxing. If on the other hand one was just to leave it be, it would enjoy a sniff and a nosy around and then leave decorously by the same way it came in. No damage done, no energy wasted and no unpleasant memories to mar the horizon until the next visit.

As I cycled past the sea of sun-bleached yellows and withered greens of Bangladesh it occurred to me that I was clinging onto dancing in anticipation of feeling lost and depressed if it was no longer part of my life. I was so used to having this passion, this undeviating and rigid path, that the thought of a life without it seemed a sort of personal Armageddon. And yet everything was telling me to move on, to venture to pastures new and spread my wings. I could not expect the transition to be easy, without doubt I would feel lost and directionless. But it needn't all be doom and gloom, floundering might be interesting for a while until slowly the new bricks of my city are laid.

So I suppose I could say I felt liberated that morning, I felt liberated from the fear of what might be in my future. The pick 'n' mix of experiences of life, I would enjoy the sweet and endure the bitter.

However, as far as the immediate future was concerned, my new reflections had yet to have the chance to filter into my habitual responses. I was about to encounter a horrible twenty-four hours.

Just as we were beginning to think the Border Security Force didn't patrol this part of the border we heard a voice shouting to us from the hill above. We looked up and saw a rifle pointing at us through one of the holes of a look-out post.

'OK! Same tactics as before everybody,' said Lee.

As you can tell we had become very blasé with the stiff arm of the law.

'Hello, *namaste,*' we chorused again, our faces adopting the same benign smiles.

'Here are our passports. We have permission to use this road.'

'Who gave you permission?' The officer said.

This was a man of obvious importance, he had a host of badges on his uniform and a more commanding presence than the cowboys down the road. We all instinctively knew not to offer him a cigarette.

'Head office back at Maheskola.'

'You have stamp?'

'No, we were given permission over the radio.'

'Please, come up to the camp.'

I don't know what came over me but I started to have a tantrum, stamping my feet on the road like an aggrieved child. I was fed up with this pointless officialdom; it was only a road. Why all the fuss?

'No!' I said defiantly whilst Tim's and Lee's heads snapped round in astonishment.

'We can't come up to the camp, we don't have enough time. Please…we have a long way to go today, just let us carry on.'

'Please madam, not to be getting angry. Only five minutes of your time.'

'Do you promise only five minutes?'

Indians have a curious way of nodding their head, it is neither a definite movement from side to side nor is it a straight up and down, rather more the chin drawing small figures of eight. I think they have cultivated this so that their affirmations cannot be held against them at a later date.

Scowling, I pushed my bike up the hill to the camp, my insightful mood of earlier rudely replaced by anger. We were repeatedly interrogated with the age-old questions and then left alone. After a while we were offered tea - just as I had suspected, it was not going to be five minutes.

The set-up was the same as the outpost camp near Baghmara: a couple of long bamboo huts for the living quarters, a kitchen hut, a shrine, a hut for the radio transmitter and a look-out post from where you could see miles of the Bangladeshi border laid out below.

Chairs were put out for us under the shade of the lookout post. One by one the soldiers made a pretence of scanning the horizon. Once their curiosity was satisfied they resumed their midday activities: boot polishing, chatting, resting.

The midday sun burned down on the camp, the air was stifling, heavy with the prospect of tedium and thick with the responsibility of wasting young men's lives. They were held hostage as much as we were, secluded from the world with no outside contact. They were allowed home once a year, travelling to Rajasthan, to Nagarland, to Orissa, their one chance to surrender to sexual desires and family love.

We watched a group of them prepare to go on duty. They stepped into army fatigues and put on jackets over thin white T-shirts, kneeling down to tie the laces on their boots. They buckled wide leather belts around their waists and hoisted rifles over their shoulders in a concert of jangling metal. They lined up in front of the radio transmitter hut, standing to attention. When our officer came out they saluted then walked down the hill with purposeful strides, the chains of the rifles clinking in time with their steps.

The camp fell silent apart from the sound of two cooks who were leaning against the kitchen hut throwing stones into the clearing and talking intermittently. We set up a self-time photo but our cameras were taken from us.

'No pictures in the camp,' a soldier yelled at us. The situation was not going our way.

Five minutes had turned into two hours and no moves seemed to be made for our release. I had a feeling that things weren't all as they should be. The officer who hauled us in was not in a position to then let us carry on. He had to wait for a signal from the headquarters in Shillong and there seemed to be a problem in getting through to them on the radio. I looked at him accusingly.

'But you promised sir, you said five minutes then we could go. You don't understand the importance of time, we take a lot longer on bicycles and we have to get the last boat crossing otherwise we are stuck in the middle of nowhere for the night.'

His English was limited, I don't know if he understood what I was saying but he didn't reply, resorting instead to that old figure of eight ruse.

Another hour passed. More soldiers from the platoon returned from duty. They lined up in front of the radio transmitter hut like the group before and performed the same procedures. They changed out of their uniforms and wandered the camp in *lungis* and flip-flops going down to the oil drum of water at the bottom of the hill to wash, towels draped around their necks, soap boxes in their hands.

Tim and Lee were doing calculations. If they let us go in the next twenty minutes we could make it if we cycled like bats out of hell. I burst into tears. This was not what it was supposed to be like, another day of racing the daylight, heart in mouth at the importance of reaching our destination by nightfall for fear of getting attacked.

Twenty minutes went by, then half an hour and then an hour. Well that was that, we had no chance of catching the boat. What were we going to do now? Why were they keeping us here all this time? I tried to read but my eyes swam with tears of hopelessness; I tried to write but could only stare out over the plains feeling sick with apprehension.

Another hour passed and they gave us some food on tin plates. Something was afoot in the camp, everybody had embarked on a fever of activity and the place had taken on an air of immediacy. The officer was shouting terse commands to his soldiers, some of whom swept the clearing while others made sure the huts were tidy. We were moved from the outpost and made to sit in a row in the clearing as if waiting to hear some verdict. The soldiers who weren't on patrol lined up outside their huts.

The reason for the furore arrived a short time afterwards. A shiny Land Rover flying the Indian flag entered the camp and a fat, important looking Singh got out. The platoon stood to attention whilst he conversed in hushed tones with our officer, looking over to us every so often with the utmost disdain. He was the Commanding Chief of the Border Security Force, bearing his rank with an imperiousness verging on farcical. He appeared to me in those first few minutes to be the most repellent man I had ever had the displeasure to meet.

He waddled over to us followed by a soldier carrying a glass of steamed milk on a tray.

'I have a bad stomach,' he said to us as if this was somehow our fault. He had a fat stomach that was all.

'What the bluddy hell do you think you are doing here?'

He was a man of few words and even less charm. We told him our story. We explained to him that we wanted to explore the unknown beauty of Meghalaya and we wanted to do it on bicycles because that was how we liked to travel.

'But why this road? I cannot believe that you are on this road for pleasure. There are plenty of other roads in Meghalaya just as beautiful as this one. If you were in Bangladesh they would put you behind bluddy bars.' His voice was rising in anger, his turban quivering in admonishment.

Over and over again we explained to him our reasons, there were no subversive motives, we were just tourists on bicycles.

The celebrity status that we had been enjoying since arriving in Meghalaya had turned against us - they now thought us spies, and even more outlandish, weapons' smugglers. Did they seriously think we had a couple of AK47's stashed in our panniers?

Our interrogation lasted for three hours in which time he wanted our education details, our jobs back home, our salaries and a list of countries we had visited in our lifetimes. Tim was servile, Lee belligerent, as for myself, I was rigid with fear. I was well aware of the ridiculousness of the situation, that we had done nothing wrong except come the wrong way and yet these men were an unknown entity capable of putting us behind 'bluddy bars' for no other reason than that they didn't know what else to do with us.

It grew dark. They cleared a hut and put up three army camp beds in a row. The light from the kerosene lamp projected our shadows, larger than life, onto the bamboo walls. Mosquitoes flew in through the opening.

I walked down to the oil drum to wash the dirt and tearstains from my face, hoping that the mere action of doing something normal might make the day seem less surreal. I plunged my hands into the drum and cupped the water to my face. Once I started I couldn't stop, the water seemed to soothe some of my distress. I rolled up my sleeves and sank my arms in far as they would go. There was a small tin sitting on a nearby rock, I took my shoes off and sloshed tin after tin of water over my feet.

The entire galaxy seemed on show that night, twinkling and glittering with a brilliance I had never witnessed before. I heard a rustle close by and froze. A soldier, sent to keep an eye on me, was making me aware of his presence, alerting me in case I intended to disrobe further and cause us both embarrassment. The metal on his rifle winked at me, my chest contracted; shit, they were taking this seriously. He kept a close distance behind as I walked back up the hill to the camp.

Supper had been delivered to the hut and the boys were tucking in to floury *rotis* and an impossibly hot curry. They appeared not to have lost their appetites, my stomach was too knotted to even contemplate it. We were even escorted to have a pee, the very knowledge turning my bladder into the size of a peanut so it seemed that every fifteen minutes the soldier on duty had to follow me to the hut at the back of the camp. I felt degraded.

Mr Singh came in to tell us he was staying in the camp especially to look after us. He was sly and untrustworthy. Afterwards they took the lamp away and we were left with no other option than to go to bed. I knew I wouldn't sleep.

We weren't even left alone to go to sleep, every half-hour flashlights were shone in our faces.

'MAPS.' We handed them over.

The next time, 'PASSPORTS.'

Lee was plugged into his radio, they took that from him too. Being separated from your passport in an army camp in the middle of nowhere did not bode well for a peaceful night's sleep. I lay awake looking at the soldiers who stopped to peer in at us as they passed the opening to our hut.

Fatman Singh got on the radio in the transmitter hut next door and for a painstaking hour he relayed all the information we had given. He spelt out every single word - twice.

'Dey - T. H. E. Y. - Tango, Hotel, Echo, Yankie. Are - A. R. E. - Alpha, Romeo, Echo. Travellers - T. R. A. V. E. L. L. E. R. S. - Tango, Romeo, Alpha...'

And so on. I found myself trying to pre-empt the international code until eventually his monotonous litany sent me to sleep. Throughout the night flashlights were shone in as they rummaged through our belongings.

We awoke at 5.30 feeling wretched and consigned to spending the next day in captivity. Our questions went unanswered. We continued sitting and waiting. Eventually Mr Singh materialised and sat himself under the look-out post with his glass of steamed milk. The previous night I could smell whisky on his breath, his bad stomach was from years of being pandered to, his every desire materialising in front of him.

We were summoned to his table and told that under no circumstances were we allowed to continue. We had to retrace our steps back to Guwahati. Finn's words rang true, *"Once you're on the road there is no going back."* Well there was for us.

I thought of the ground we had already covered, the roads that were stained with our sweat and a wave of exhaustion engulfed me. Going back was not an option we could take. We tried one last time to get permission but our pleas fell on deaf ears. They knew all along they wouldn't let us, we were kept in the camp all that time for their enjoyment and to remind them that they had the power to intimidate and control. I hated them with a vengeance. To add insult to injury we were made to sign a form declaring that we had been treated well and respectfully. It was only later that we found out they had been through all of our belongings and stolen some things that took their fancy. We fell on our passports like asthmatics to ventilators and held our heads high as we cycled down the hill out of the camp.

The relief of being free. The problems we now faced were of no concern to us in those first few moments after our release. The adrenaline that had been stored up in our bodies over the last twenty-four hours came flooding out as we hared along the road back to Maheskola, wanting to put as much distance between the camp and us as fast as possible.

We arrived back in the village panting. The relief had passed and the enormity of what lay ahead hit us full and square in the face. We were a day and a half away from Shillong if only we could carry on, we were eight days away if we had to go back. Glenna was arriving in Guwahati in two days time.

'There has to be another road to the river,' said Lee.

'There must be, the border road looks relatively new and the trucks would have had to get to Ranikor somehow,' Tim agreed.

They poured over every inch of the map.

'Look! What's that? It looks like a track running through the jungle and it's following the lines of the border road. That must have been what they used.'

'I think you could be right. Fanbloodytastic! Our problems could be solved. Come on, let's go to the local police and ask them.'

I wanted nothing more to do with the authorities around these parts but we couldn't venture off into the unknown without some more information.

It turned out to be somewhat unsatisfactory. We had interrupted a game of cards and our second coming to the village did not hold the same allure. As usual everyone had something to say but little could be understood. Some seemed to be saying that the road was in too bad a condition for bicycles, others, from what we could decipher, reckoned it was OK. We asked the distance.

'Twenty-six kilometres.'

'*Acha*, fifty-eight kilometres.'

'No no no please, thirty-seven kilometres but be careful – "Tiger".'

To our utmost relief a lot of them didn't agree. I put my hand up to my heart to tell it to calm down when a man piped up from the corner, 'Yes, tiger - but only night.'

'Well that's alright then,' said Lee. 'We'll be in Ranikor by dark.'

'Hang on a minute, let's not be hasty, there might be another way. I really don't want to cycle through the middle of the jungle not knowing how far it is to the river. We might get attacked by a tiger.'

I never thought I would ever have the occasion to use that last sentence. It sounded so alien on my lips that I had to say it again, 'We might get attacked by a tiger guys.'

'Polly we don't have time to discuss it and we don't have a choice. It's either carry on or cycle all the way back to Dainadubi,' said Tim.

'Come on. We'll keep a steady pace, have lots of rests. We can do it no problem.' Lee was full of confidence.

It was midday when we set off. We cycled through the village, passed the turning for the border road and onwards to the forested hills that lay ahead. The condition of the road became steadily worse until, by the time we were in the jungle, jagged boulders lay strewn across the track. The track and the roots of the trees seemed locked in a constant battle for supremacy. Sometimes the path held the upper hand, at other places the roots spread out conquering the stones and forming a gnarled staircase. We rode, then we pushed, then rode again, then got off and pushed some more. Our progress was painstakingly slow. All I could see was a never-ending range of jungled hills, no clearings or villages to ease the eye or reassure the heart. I couldn't do it, I just couldn't do it.

'Come on Polly, yes you can. You're a strong woman, you're

physically able.' The boys tried to instill me with confidence.

Every so often the path gave way to rickety bridges that appeared in the twilight years of their lives. A couple of the planks seemed strong, the others seemed to cling to existence whilst large patches rotted and crumbled away falling into the deep ravine below. We passed two villagers coming in the opposite direction carrying sacks of fruit on their backs and knives tucked into their belts. They told us we had taken the wrong road. I couldn't do it, I just couldn't do it.

'Come on Polly, you're doing great. Don't waste your energy on thinking that. Take each kilometre at a time. We'll be fine, we'll get there.'

My nerves were fraught with the last sequence of events and I had a sick, hollow feeling in the pit of my stomach. I could not seem to disassociate the situation at hand from the situation with Tim and our future together. I didn't know if I was blaming him for putting me through this, all I knew as I pushed my bike behind him was that I couldn't make the decision to follow him to New Zealand. Every cell in my body wished to be home, like I had never wished for it before and yet it seemed a million light years away from here.

Is this what a life with Tim would be like? A future of intrepid journeys, physical tests, emotional upheaval? If that were the case then he had picked the wrong woman and I had picked the wrong man. Could we have got it horribly wrong? Had we really only gone twelve kilometres in two hours? I wasn't going to make it, I just wasn't.

My arms had lost all strength to push, I got back on the saddle. No sooner had I got back on than I hit a stone at a wrong angle and came crashing to the ground, bruising my hip and cutting my arms and legs on the sharp rocks. I started to cry, huge wracking sobs that echoed out into the stillness of the jungle. I could not seem to stem my anguish and my arms flailed uncontrollably as if gripped by an epileptic fit.

Tim came to me immediately and clamped his arms around me trying to calm me down. I couldn't breathe, I couldn't speak, I didn't know what to do with myself. We sat like that for ages, Tim stroking my hair and whispering a ceaseless stream of reassurances in my ear until I had calmed down enough to speak. The words came out jumbled and disorientated.

'I'm too tired to carry on...I can't be with you...I just want to go home...there is no future for us Tim.'

I had lost all perspective of what was really distressing me. Meghalaya had seemed to be one long test of character and I felt I had endured enough.

'Don't give up on me now Polly, I love you too much.' Tim cupped my face and stared into my eyes. 'It's alright, we're turning back, we'll find another way. Come on, don't worry any more.'

He ran ahead to find Lee who had carried on. A while later they both appeared discussing the next plan of action. Lee understood my desire to turn back but his concern was for reaching Glenna in time and he had a bee in his bonnet about proving something to the bastards at the Border Security Force. As if they would ever know, let alone care. Tim suggested that maybe Lee should carry on without us and we meet him back in Guwahati. We came to the conclusion that it was best we stick together; it seemed hard enough to travel as a threesome let alone by oneself.

We turned around and embarked on the long walk back. I knew that if it wasn't for me they would have carried on. This was the first time that my gender was an issue. I knew I was not physically or mentally strong enough to push my bike along that track for another thirty kilometres. But why did my physical handicap have to fail me now, just when I needed most to be one of the boys? Perhaps they were secretly relieved that I called the shots that day, who knows what we would have encountered if we had carried on.

But our guardian angels were hovering near. Not more than two kilometres later we heard the rumble of a distant engine. Could it be a truck? More likely a scooter. We waited eagerly scanning the horizon for a glimpse of something. The sound got louder and louder until a battered truck lumbered around the bend. We leapt in front waving our arms like mad. Not only was it heading back to Williamnagar but also this time its cargo was hay. Could it be that we might get a comfortable ride for once? It transpired that the truck did that journey once a week although not for much longer, the conditions were too bad and the damage to the truck too severe. We threw the bikes in the back and nestled our bums into the hay laughing with relief at our outrageous fortune.

The journey took hours and the soft hay was not all it promised to be. Within minutes the sharp edges of each blade cut our bodies to pieces. No matter, rather that than militants or tigers. I was lucky and after a time managed to secure a place in the cab. The bumping and screeching Hindi music rocked me to sleep like a mother's lullaby and as I closed my eyes I could not resist my head from resting against the shoulder of a young local woman cradling her new born baby.

By nightfall we had returned to Williamnagar, our lacerations stinging and bleary-eyed with exhaustion. We limped to the local police station to try and get somewhere to stay. It was a problem, the circuit house was full of visiting missionaries. All we wanted was to lie flat, all the Superintendent wanted was to ply us with betel nut and tea. Well up for any kind of buzz, we thought it was probably as good a time as any to try. I can only describe it as chewing on walnut shells mixed with Vim. My mouth contorted with involuntary spasms.

'Keep going,' said Tim, 'It gets better.'

No it didn't. It was without doubt the most disgusting thing I

172

had ever put in my mouth. I ran outside and spat it out.

Tim came out and started snooping around the garden of the police station. In the corner under a tree lay an upturned rowing boat. In monsoon time it had been known to become so flooded that the boat was needed to get from place to place. In the winter however, it had another purpose. Tim lifted it up and found a stash of empty liquor bottles underneath.

'Ah, your officers have been drinking I see,' he said to the Superintendent.

'Yes, it is necessary. Without drinking the officers cannot do their job properly.' He replied with no sense of irony.

The labels read "Officers Choice" and on the back in small print it said "Defence Whisky - Only For Consumption by Defence Services." So the police and army wages were supplemented with free liquor courtesy of the Indian government. Well, that explained quite a lot.

Eventually a policeman arrived and said accommodation had been found but he stressed it was very basic. As long as no soldiers shone torches in my face throughout the night then any shack would seem palatial.

We found out that a bus was leaving at 5.30 the following morning heading in the direction of Guwahati. From there we could try to get another bus or pay a driver to take us into the city. Things seemed bright, we were going to make it in time.

The following morning we sat squished in another biscuit tin on wheels. The boys had perfected the procedure of getting our bikes strapped onto the roof although it was an attribute not readily welcomed when reminded of the cycling odyssey this was intended to be. The mist lay thick in the valley as the moody views rolled past the window, the sun now coming to greet us in a sliver of deep orange cutting through the fog.

Goodbye Meghalaya - land of cloud and perpetual wind, land of the little people abiding simply, hand in hand with exaggerated beauty. Resist the bait to enter the twentieth century, remain innocent in destroying our planet, keep your doors unlocked and your windows open so that your trust in human beings lives on. It has a long way to go until it is ready to welcome tourists, but no doubt it will happen as the urge for human discovery probes ever deeper into all corners of the world. Good or bad? Right or wrong? We could argue forever. If my presence caused disquiet or intrusion then I humbly apologise. If my presence excited or entertained then I am glad. The remoteness of Meghalaya stripped me of some layers and challenged some senses. I felt present - my steps not taken to reach a destination nor to get away. I wanted only to walk.

13

TWO WEEKS LATER. DELHI - THE BRITISH EMBASSY

'Sorry - tell me again, where have you been?'

'Cycling around Assam.'

The British diplomat looked clearly alarmed. He kept shaking his head and tutting. 'If we knew of your intentions we would never have let you go. Do you realise how dangerous Assam is? Next to Papua New Guinea it is the second most dangerous place to be for gratuitous homicide.' (The Balkans had yet to flare up again).

'We were aware to a certain extent, we just didn't appreciate the gravity of the situation.'

He shook his head again, looking bemused. He had the pallor of someone who goes from an air-conditioned office to an air-conditioned gym and then on to the air-conditioned Embassy bar to eat Walkers crisps and read the Daily Mail whilst the clamour of India goes by unnoticed.

'No, you obviously didn't. Well, you're very lucky, it could have been quite another story.'

Looking back from the safety of my home I still cannot believe the naive trust we had when we embarked on our tour of Assam. The story I am about to tell I feel should come with a Blue Peter style warning - PLEASE DO NOT TRY AT THIS HOME! Or not unless you thrive on danger or take a masochistic enjoyment in fearing for the safety of your life. But, to make a tenuous comparison with all who were involved in the World Wars, living with danger brings with it its own sweet mixture of a heightened existence. A hug becomes an embrace, a snack becomes a feast, a short distance travelled becomes a conquest.

My grandmother, like many women of her generation, thrived on the consequences of World War II. A diminutive woman with an over-sized personality and ceaseless energy, she worked before the war as a seamstress in London. When war broke out her only child, my father, was evacuated to a butcher's family in Northamptonshire. Relieved of the burdens of motherhood, for it was apparent that was how she perceived it, and fed-up with chivvying an idle husband, she signed herself up as an ambulance driver.

In the height of The Blitz, my grandmother blossomed as she drove her ambulance through the streets of London. Suddenly her life was purposeful and vibrant, the constant parting and uniting was either unbearable or joyful but never dull, and even the tension was cosy and companionable.

In the two weeks of travelling in Assam fear took up residence in my body. I courted it in the morning, in the afternoon, in the evening and went to sleep with it at night. But like my grandmother I felt suffused with a radiant well-being so that when the golden ball of sun sank behind a bamboo thicket and a glimpse of a bright pink sari crossed our path, I felt in those moments addicted to adventure and I wanted it to last forever.

"With all the power of my arms,

With all the intelligence of my mind,

With all the loves of my heart,

I pay due respect to you, the soul within."

Hindu translation for Namaste

14
DENIM AND GINGER

It was easy to forget the danger in the glorious and grotesque abundance of Guwahati. The fetid and chaotic streets were strangely soothing after the remoteness of the Meghalayan hills. As I crossed the city I felt curiously at home.

The gutters lay thick with rubbish. What wasn't consumed by the working classes was tossed outside for the beggars, what wasn't recycled by the beggars was left for the cats and dogs, what they didn't eat the goats devoured and whatever they left behind was picked over by the rats and cockroaches. One could say it was the perfect eco-system. The problems arise when the rains come. The streets have no drainage and as the water levels rise the buoyant rubbish begins an aimless journey through the city bringing with it sickness and disease.

I walked for hours through the stalls of the Fancy Bazaar gazing at the kaleidoscopic display of silks hanging in the windows or rolled up like bolsters and packed onto shelves. How would you ever choose? Assamese silk is a rich and rare fabric worn only by the ladies of high society. They come in threes to discuss and prevaricate, holding metres of luxury up to their faces in a melody of giggles and jangling bracelets. The shopkeeper flatters and fawns, sweeping clean the padded floor for them to sit on and ordering tea from his boy Friday. These types of women I saw later coming out of the English Boarding School on Bordoloi Road looking exquisite as they held on to the hands of their children, dressed in white knee-length socks and holding exercise books. They were unconcerned that the hems of their expensive saris scraped along the dirt of the street, they were nonplused by the limbless beggars that held out their hands to them entreatingly. There are no dividing districts in this city, rich reside with poor, lavish wealth next to recoiling poverty. India is a country of conflicting realities. Does one try to make sense of it or does one just submerge and experience?

We had work to do in Guwahati. We needed permission again to stay in the government-run Circuit Houses and Inspection Bungalows. Lee went to the airport to meet Glenna and Tim and I went to find the Select Committees. Again it turned out to be an isometric test of corridors and manila files but the people we approached were courteous and helpful and, with the mention of travelling by bicycle, we were awarded an instant show of respect. They promised to make the appropriate telephone calls and nodded and shook their heads in the comforting manner that we had grown accustomed to, neither promising one thing or forbidding another. We were given a letter and we had faith that we would land on our feet. The letter read:

"A group of adventurists from the UK and Newzeland will be visiting different places of ecological importance in Assam on by-cyle from this week. You are requested to render all possible assistance to them for performing their tour comfortably as and when approached."

Signed: The Acting Chief Engineer to the Deputy Officer of the Sub-divisional Roads Planning Corporation of Assam, Guwahati.

We were anticipating long, flat roads running alongside the banks of the Brahmaputra, tea gardens in front of us and behind, wildlife reserves full of rhino and elephants and all of this yet to be exploited by tourism.

'And as for the food,' Finn had told us in the pub back in London, 'you are never going to eat food like you will in Assam. They will ply you with food like you won't be able to imagine and it is delicious. Oh, and the tea, you are never going to drink so much tea in your lives either, you won't want to look at the stuff again when you get home.'

Good food and the promise of elephants, suddenly the prospect of travelling seemed rosy and exciting again. I was also to have a female ally to add to our entourage. I couldn't wait to see Glenna, I realised how much I had missed another female's company. Tim and I had twelve days left together before I caught the train to Delhi and he flew to Calcutta. I was determined not to dwell on our imminent parting, even though I was now in the equivalent of the final category of my school holiday – the MAJOR DREAD category.

'Polly, you have grown up.' I kept repeating to myself in the hope that by endless repetition it would begin to take effect. I knew I had grown up but some things take a long time to die. Tears welled up in my eyes every time we passed the train station at the very thought of what it would be like next time we were inside.

Before meeting Lee and Glenna at the hotel we went for a snack at the street corner stall we had eaten breakfast in that morning. We wanted to savour every minute of our time alone together, we hadn't had any for such a long time. I loved this food stall with a passion, it was by far the best place in town to get a cup of tea and fresh *samosas*. All the rickshaw drivers thought so too, they also came here to fuel their legs.

So seamless was the operation it was like watching kinetic art. The tea man mashed ginger with the base of a glass whilst boiling milk and sugar on the Primus stove and adding more tea leaves to a saucepan of water. He carried out this three-step manoeuvre dodging the *samosa* man who was crouched down on an upturned bucket cutting out triangle after triangle of pastry. The chief was in charge of frying the *samosas* as well as spooning out ladles of *chana* into little stainless steel bowls and handing them out to a constant flow of rickshaw peddlers. Each man had his role; seven days a week they took up their positions, never swapping for a change of scene to relieve the boredom. It was a mesmerising and beautiful performance to watch, everything utilised and not a superfluous action taken. Tim was most impressed, he said it was more slick and professional than any highly acclaimed restaurant he had worked in.

Our anonymity at the stall did not last for long. We noticed a chunky Indian dressed head to toe in denim, with a pair of Ray-Bans perched sassily on his nose, making his way towards us. He had the air of someone who liked to impart knowledge whether it was wanted or not. He asked us what we were doing here.

'Cycling? You do not want to do that man. It's a jungle out there man, I tell you it's a jungle.'

Yeah so! We had just come from a jungle or did he mean metaphorically?

'They are evil mothers man, they have no mercy these people out here. I tell you I get real scared when I come up here, real scared.'

He had obviously spent time in LA or had watched a lot of Die Hards.

'So why do you come?'

'Business. I export ginger. Do you know where ginger grows? I'll tell you. It grows in the most out of the way places, in the wild. I have men who work for me, who go and harvest it but man I've had so many threats, I'm telling you death threats. It's just a matter of time before something happens and I gotta get out of here before it's too late. The tribals, they think nothing of chopping your head off.'

I could sense Tim willing him to stop as I froze beside him. I had just got rid of my foreboding and now it had come back with even more force than before.

'Listen, we're after no one's ginger, we're just touring. We'll be at our destination before dark. I don't think we're a target for the militants.'

'Yeah, you're probably OK, but then again you never know. Just be careful, you know what I'm saying?'

He left. We rationalised. He was a fat cat businessman from Delhi making a lot of money from exploiting a natural plant. It was obvious that he was not going to be popular with the locals. We would just have to put that little incident from our minds.

Back at the hotel I fell on Glenna like a long lost friend. It was so refreshing to look at and hear another person's stories, even her cycling kit was of interest, so bored were we of looking at each other in our scruffy clothes. That night we were full of excitement, toasting to our onward journey and to the new recruit on board.

"I will be the waves and you will be the shore.

I shall roll on and on, and break upon your

lap with laughter. And no one in the world will

know where we both are."

Rabindranath Tapore

15
BALOO! I THINK I LOVE YOU

Here we were again, setting off in the early morning, the thrill of the unknown ahead, the knowledge that everything we would need we had packed in our panniers. The pleasure of existing with so few possessions was intense. I had noticed a pattern of behaviour in myself in the recent years. Returning home after a long tour or a stint abroad I would throw out bin-liners full of clothes and odds and ends. The weeks spent in sterile hotel rooms seemed to purge my need for clutter and I found shelves full of knick-knacks claustrophobic.

I thought I had all but the bare essentials in my panniers but if I was ruthless I still carried things that I could live without like my dress and my lipstick and my mouthwash. These meagre items represented the last vestiges of my femininity but even in this briefest of sojourns from my normal life I could not quite bring myself to discard them. They stayed at the bottom of my panniers just in case I was called upon to look pretty. The occasion was only called for once but still it was worth toiling with them up and down mountains for the security and the comfort. Part of me was amused by this trait but a big part was slightly vexed that I didn't have the confidence to do without my social armour for seven weeks of my life.

My shopping habits, when viewed from the monastic existence I was living, seemed absurdly extravagant. Does the money I spend on a pair of suede boots really equate with the heady pleasure I get from knowing that I am the owner of these exquisite things that hug my ankle so becomingly and flatter my foot? Absolutely - for about a day and a half anyway. They then become commonplace like the boots bought last year for near enough the same reasons and no doubt like the ones I shall buy two months from now which I anticipate will add to my quality of life immeasurably. My father takes great pride in still wearing the shoes that he bought on his twenty-first birthday.

'But Dad, they don't make them like that anymore.'

This is true, but even if they did, imagine the tedium. If you live in a city, or anywhere big enough to have a Ritzy's nightclub, then the social structure dictates that you need at least five different outfits to go out in, a large selection of work clothes, weekend wear plus a few wedding, funeral, christening, garden party, Wimbledon and Henley Regatta numbers as well. Additionally, you need gym gear which differs ever so subtly from your Yoga kit which is white and floppy as opposed to lycra and stripey.

I was enjoying this respite from the pressures of fashion. It reminded me of my school days when getting dressed meant leaning over to the chair beside my bed and putting on my uniform that I had worn the day before and the day before and the year before and the year before that. But the need for individuality, the basic desire to feel attractive, is a strong human quality of the female persona. At the weekend, when we were allowed to change into home clothes after lunch, the amount of forward planning which went into our outfits was really quite astonishing. We would start assimilating what we were going to wear on Wednesday. It would start with a brief chat after lights out, perhaps entailing booking an item of clothing from a friend.

'Annabel, can I borrow your polka dot ra-ra skirt on Saturday please?'

'No, I said Sammy Harker could wear it.'

'But I'm your best friend.'

'Yeah, but she said I could borrow her ankle boots.'

'God, well thanks for being loyal. Not.'

Animosity would pervade the dormitory for a couple of days.

What are best friends for if not to have first refusal on your ra-ra skirt? Friday night we would have a try-on session ready for the big day on Saturday. Interestingly there weren't even any boys to dress up for (God help us if there were). There was nowhere to go but amble around the cavernous corridors of the mansion house. Come supper time at six o'clock we weren't allowed into the dining-room in short skirts or trousers and so we had to slip on our Character skirts (used for dancing classes) over the top of our jumbo cord drain-pipes that we had been dreaming about wearing for four days. It was our chance during those weekend afternoons to break out from feeling like an androgynous clone and in the very name - home clothes - it seemed to bring home a little closer if only the lingering smell of Mum's washing powder.

I knew that the simple pleasure of choosing between pair of cycling shorts number one and two would not continue once I was back home. But the more do we find ourselves obsessing upon the body then surely something as important as our soul becomes neglected.

The road out of Guwahati was noisy and polluted. It was also exceedingly dull except for a brief interlude when we cycled past a field full of vultures. After a few hours we stopped for the obligatory tea break. It occurred to me then that a large proportion of my life had been centred around the tea break event. BTB or ATB, Before Tea Break or After Tea Break, were phrases said regularly throughout the course of my average working day. How much you look forward to your tea break equates to how much responsibility you hold at work. If you find yourself counting down the minutes then you either don't hold much clout in the company or you're bored and unchallenged. The tea break event is especially important when it is dictated by someone else, this is when you really know you are nothing but a minion. Alternatively, in a dance company for instance, you know you have made it when you call the tea break shots.

'OK guys, let's run it from the top twice more before a tea break and if you do it well enough, and by that I mean no mistakes, high energy and lots of style, then you only have to do it once. After tea break we will learn some more and then go back to the top again. Alright? Is everyone clear?'

This was when we would turn to Alex, who was not blessed with great rhythm and counting abilities.

'Alex! Get the counts right on the allegro otherwise we'll have to do it again and it will be your fault.'

How come this guy is a dancer you may ask. He looked fantastic in a pair of tights. It was a good ploy of the rehearsal assistant; suddenly everyone's stomachs were held in, eyes on stalks trying to stay in line and on the beat whilst heads were full of one thing only:

'Shall I have tea...maybe I'll have a cappuccino. Ooh, I am gasping for a fag. Do I have time to run and get a Mars I wonder? Nearly at the end...jump and a jump and finish on the knee. Phew...a rest!'

'Sorry people, it's not good enough yet. One more time. Alex! Get on the music.'

'WHAT! She can't be serious!' The hatred directed at the rehearsal assistant at that moment was enough to start World War III. Relax everyone it's only a tea break.

More often than not it was Lee who dictated when we had our tea breaks as normally he cycled way ahead of us. We did try yelling down the road but it was uncouth and impractical because he never chose to hear. A great deal of my time in India was spent willing Lee to get thirsty or tired and, similar to rehearsals, I found my head consumed with one thing …TEA BREAK.

Glenna's reaction to our stops in the tea shack was one of bewilderment and surprise. We had grown accustomed to the staring and the overcrowding but there is no doubt about it - at first it unnerves. The Assamese had one thing that their fellow countrymen did not - an autograph book. From this point on our tea breaks took on a new dimension. Not only did we have to contend with curious stares but now we had to write our addresses and short bon mots in book after book after book. In an accumulative frenzy sometimes the owner would push his book in front of our noses a second time.

'Look! You already have my address.'

'Please madam, please to be having it again. Just for to be making sure.'

Icarumba! It would then turn into a photographic shoot, the one camera in the village dusted and demothed. The combinations went like this. Tim and Lee with the important men of the village, Glenna and I with the women. Tim and Lee with the important men of the village's wives, Glenna and I with the children. Tim and Lee with the important men of the village, the important men's wives, and their sons, Glenna and I with the adolescent girls. Tim and Lee with the newborn baby sons, Glenna and I with the village goats. It took an hour to pass through each village. Just as we were about to ride off again a left-out autograph book would have to be signed and one last photo taken. It was wonderfully exasperating.

We rode on inhaling alarming quantities of the thick diesel fumes that pumped out of the trucks and buses that raced past us continuously. The drivers, always keen to have a look at us, came perilously close and hooted their horn continuously. Hang on a minute, where were the deserted roads and the unspoiled beauty of Assam? The scenery was vapid and the road bumpy, uneven and crowded.

Feeling frazzled and very dirty we arrived at the small town of Mangaldai well before dark. We went straight to the police station to confirm our rooms at the Circuit House. Indian bureaucracy had failed us this time. The message in Guwahati had not been forwarded, we were back to telling our story once more. I was beginning to learn not to worry about accommodation, it was only a matter of time, it was only a matter of endless cups of tea and chit-chat and jokes before the wheels were set in motion. The Indians don't want to waste an opportunity to bestow their hospitality or to catch up on news of their relations.

'I have an uncle in England. He has a very, very nice restaurant in Birmingham. Perhaps you know him?'

We were taken past the village green where a cricket game was taking place, in fact on every spare bit of grass throughout the whole of India cricket was probably being played. It was the cricket World Cup and the subcontinent was gripped in batting fever. I liked it, it made the world seem a smaller place - the global inspiration of sport. My father has a theory that if an Englishman were to travel anywhere in the world and ask someone what he or she knew of England the reply would always be the same - Manchester United and Princess Diana. I put his theory to the test later that afternoon on a guard who was watching me as I read.

'What do you associate with England?'

He didn't hesitate in his reply, 'Mr Bean, he is very very funny yes?'

No, he is not. He is an irritating dweeb that has managed to ingratiate himself world-wide. If an Argentinean was to ask me the same question I would answer Che Guvara and steak. Likewise with a Kiwi - Kire Te Kanawa and the All Blacks, for France it would have to be the Marquis de Sade and croissants, South Africa - Mandela and billtong. But what are we known for? Mr Bean. Unfortunately, the innocent guard in Mangaldai is not alone in his association; if I was to ask any one of the millions of Japanese in Tokyo they would give me

189

the same answer.

This Circuit House was particularly squalid and even in the afternoon infested with mosquitoes; huge, juicy, fat mosquitoes that had an indecent appetite for blood. Even inside our room we were unable to open our mouths for fear of one of them flying in. They clung to the ceiling in droves and scaled the mosquito net as if it were a climbing frame. We were close to the swampy breeding banks of the Brahmaputra, which to a mosquito must be like hanging out in downtown LA where sex is on offer everywhere, the air damp and sultry and loads of shit to feast upon. Within seconds my neck was eaten to pieces.

A couple of magistrates came to quiz us about our intended route. They frowned and huffed and looked very uncomfortable.

'It is too dangerous, they are merciless these people and do not adhere to any uniformity in their targets. I am thinking it is not wise for you to go.'

I have found that there is always one who doesn't say much in the main bulk of the conversation but strikes in the moment when your brain is trying to assimilate all that it has heard so far.

'Also snakes. Beware, very dangerous snakes.'

'Take no notice of him,' Tim whispered. 'He's just an old woman.'

Old woman or not, the ramifications didn't look good either way. None of it felt worth it any more. How can you travel fearing for your very safety all for the cause of adventure, just to visit a place where hardly any westerners have been and worse still because of what one man told us back in London? The whole thing felt crazy and I was not about to become a cycling pioneer. So what were the alternatives?

'The District Commissioner is coming here tonight. He will tell you what you can do.'

We sat around silent and glum. Lee was feeling ill and was lying under the mosquito net, Tim was pottering and Glenna and I were going through the merits of having adventuresome boyfriends. Could we think of any? Did the sight of their maps and compasses, their Leatherman knives that cut through bush one minute then buttered a sandwich the next make them that much more attractive to us?

In my view eighties adventure romances, especially those starring Kathleen Turner and Michael Douglas, have a lot to answer for. In the film *Romancing the Stone* Kathleen goes off into the wilds of the South American jungle to find her sister who was researching a group of long lost tribals. Sliding down a rain-soaked mud bank she just so happens to bump headlong into Michael Douglas who was running away from a fierce drug cartel. They form a reluctant duo, fleeing and escaping from the drug barons and searching for the sister, bickering and abusing one another until, having just swung over a cavernous ravine and surviving a near-death experience, they cling together under a dripping vine and declare undying passion.

Throughout their journey Kathleen remains pretty and unblemished while Michael, all torn-shirts and sweating tendrils, still manages to toss off witticisms whilst karate chopping an assailing thug and giving smouldering looks that women dream about for weeks.

For many a night afterwards I would go to bed dreaming of being Kathleen Turner running wild in the jungle and falling in love with an errant man while fleeing for my life. Well, what do you know? Here I was with all the ingredients for a Hollywood adventure story, even the Danny DeVito sidekick appears in many different guises. We had the scenery, the danger and the romance but if ever a truer word was said, 'It ain't the movies now.' Far from looking pretty I was red-nosed and spotty and Tim had lost too much weight to be described as hunky. His shirts weren't so much torn as curry stained and his jokes tended to be a bit hit or miss. Bring on the Winnebago and the make-up artist so I could affiliate myself to Kathleen Turner and maybe the outlook would have looked rosier.

The District Commissioner had arrived and we were ushered up to his overtly plush quarters. Although he was Mr Power around here it was difficult to locate him in the enormity of his armchair. He was one of the tiniest men I had ever met. What he lacked in stature he made up for in twinkling eyes and animated gestures. He spoke what he believed was perfect English, although it was hard to understand, and crossed and uncrossed his legs at the same time as waving his arms about like a conductor going through the steps of River Dance.

'Safe, safe, safe,' he said as his arms whooshed from side to side as if bringing in the wind section, then the brass and, finally, the strings.

'I will make sure you have police protection all the way to Tezpur.'

He made a few telephone calls, dictated letters to his clerk and then crossed his legs and declared it, 'Done! Go off and see this beautiful land.' He was a mover and shaker alright; we liked this man. Or we thought we liked this man.

'You (pointing to Glenna and I) would never marry in India. Your hair too short, it is not considered beautiful. You could have degree, degrees, degrees and big dowry but no man would ask you for marrying.'

He wouldn't say that if I was Kathleen Turner. Maybe that's where this trip had gone wrong, next time I would grow my hair. He asked us where our fourth person was and we told him he was ill.

'Ah, I am thinking he is puking.'

He was thinking rightly but to hear him say 'puke' was so discordant with the rest of his speech that we could not help but laugh.

192

We went back to our room but the mosquitoes were having a party which we would rather not have attended. We had no choice but to seek refuge under our nets. My head was spinning with worries, we had heard so many conflicting opinions. I did not know whether to believe the terror harbingers or the poo-pooing dismissives. I had secretly hoped that the District Commissioner would have forbade us from going, but he hadn't. Maybe things really were going to be alright. I had refused once already and made them turn back, I couldn't do it a second time.

We left the Circuit House just as it was beginning to get light. Our destination was a small place called Orang where only three days before seven people were shot dead and a bridge blown up. The Bodos were exciting pressure on the government for their independence, reminding them with a stream of dead bodies not to become complacent. Orang was the hub of the insurgencies at that moment. The Forestry Officer in Guwahati had told us that there was a wildlife sanctuary nearby, deep in the national park. It was not open for the public but if we mentioned his name we would be able to stay. It seemed far-fetched but that was our destination.

I sat rigid in my saddle as we left the safety of Mangaldai for the open road to Orang. It was chilly and quiet and mist hung in the air making the atmosphere eerie and rather depressing. We cycled alongside flat fields and murky rivers, passing people pulling vegetable carts and workhands heading for the tea gardens. The road was bad and with each jolt my back felt like it was being drained of all its spinal fluid. I expected every passing truck to throw out a net and scoop us up or balaclava-wearing bandits to jump out of the teahouses. Glenna and I beseeched the guys not to race off. Instead we cycled like a well-trained regiment, two ahead side by side, two close behind. I can't remember much of the scenery, I kept my head down and dared not look anyone in the eye. Where the hell was our police escort anyway? Don't tell me Mr Power was just another ham sandwich without the ham.

We could cover vast amounts of ground in a short time when we put our minds to it. As I have mentioned before, fear puts one hell of a kick into your muscles. We had to stop for breakfast so we picked the one tea shack which looked the least subversive. Like the beer house in Munich where Hitler and his entourage were supposed to have plotted the second World War, I wondered if any of the UFLA (United Front for the Liberation of Assam) had plotted which train to blow up next whilst eating *puris* at this very table.

The magistrates in Mangaldai warned us that the UFLA appear the friendliest people in the village. They charm you and are gracious but come nightfall or a quiet road and then they slit your throat open. This information did not make for a relaxed breakfast. We were surrounded by the usual throng of onlookers but now their smiles seemed laced with ulterior motives and the breakfast of *puris* and cauliflower curry that I had grown to love now seemed to stick in my throat.

We tried to keep the mood light but it was hard going. I felt sorry for Glenna who had not had a chance to become accustomed to life on the road, let alone one with impending danger. She had not had the gentle pace of Nepal nor the beauty of Meghalayan mornings to make it seem worthwhile.

As we were finishing our breakfast we heard a loud commotion behind us, two heavily armed trucks had just arrived in the village. Could this really be our protection? It looked more like an army training exercise than an escort. The leader of 'operation cyclists' looked like Baloo the bear from the Jungle Book. He could barely fit into his uniform, his belly was low slung and appeared to be a living amorphous entity separate from the rest of his body. He had the rather frazzled look of somebody who had spent the past few hours trying to gather his troops together. I don't think he reckoned on such an early start and now looked somewhat relieved that he had found us alive and in one piece. He had a smiling, friendly face and I wanted to jump on his big, sturdy body and give him a kiss. I knew at that instant why Whitney Houston fell in love with Kevin Costner, here was my bodyguard entrusted to keep us in the land of the living - I loved him.

And so we set off, the four of us and the twenty of them. I had a quick scan to see if any of the villagers had a look of disappointment on their faces now that their plans had been scuppered. Hah, not a bloody chance now buckoes, we've got Baloo to look after us.

We were smiling, we were singing, we were laughing, and then we were listening, and then we were obsessively listening, and then we couldn't help but listen, and then we were listening so much we wanted to scream. The drone of the engines driving right behind us, never getting further than second gear, was turning us all to distraction. For hour after endless hour the monotonous humming buzzed like flies in our ears. At times they changed down to first gear which at least provided a slightly different tone until, the bumpy patch over, we regained our speed and they changed back into second.

When we stopped for tea breaks they trundled out of the jeep. A few were ordered to stay behind and keep vigil over the bikes whilst the others hovered around us warding off curious onlookers with a stick. The amount of autographs we signed reduced drastically, when Baloo decided that we had signed enough he gave his command and the autograph books magically disappeared.

It was with a certain amount of trepidation that Glenna and I stripped down to our cycling shorts once the sun was high in the sky. We had to disrobe, we were sweating profusely. There was no alternative but to bear the consequences of having twenty lascivious policemen staring at our arses for the rest of the afternoon. When the sun shone in the right place the lycra of Glenna's shorts appeared see-through so the tempting outline of her g-string could be seen. Oh boy - were they going to have a good afternoon!

'SHIT! SHIT!'

I suddenly remembered that I wasn't wearing anything underneath. Rather distressingly we heard loud laughter and some back slapping from the front of the trucks. It sounded like they had picked a rump to fixate on for the duration of the trip. Be benevolent, Polly, they must have some perks for doing what had to be the most boring job known to man. Or was it? Maybe the conversation went more along the lines of, 'Hey what a great day! What a lovely cruisy day! No ULFA beating, no hanging round the station, just pert arses to stare at and fags to smoke. Go on have another tea break, we're in no hurry. Yippee, there's a hill coming guys, let's hope the girls stand up.'

When we eventually arrived at Orang the policemen dismounted, wreathed in smiles. Just as I thought, they were having a great day. The superintendent came out to greet us and ushered us into the teahouse where tea and syrupy sweets were placed before us. What was it with the head policemen in these parts? Here was another one who looked like a long-lost relation of James Brown: ring-laden fingers, smoothed hair, small wiry body and an ill-fitting jacket with too much shoulder pad. But it was more than his appearance, he seemed to have a gleam in his eye that was not averse to doing a spot of tax evading or bootlegging himself. He was N. R. Roy and he was at our service.

"When I appear in public people expect me to neigh, grind my teeth, paw the ground and swish my tail – none of which is easy."

Princess Anne
Observer 'Saying of the Week' 1977

16

'FIRST I MAY HAVE TO KILL A MAN'

The ride to Orang Wildlife Sanctuary was like cycling through a Walt Disney film, there was not one ugly sight; we had entered the set of *Fantasia*. We turned off the main road and followed an unpitched track heading towards the park, cycling through banana plantations and alongside rice terraces where tender new shoots were standing to attention before the sun. We passed small lakes littered with floating lotus flowers and bamboo homesteads where young children ran out to look at us, a bunch of fingers in their mouths and wearing nothing but a pair of knickers and a string of beads.

It seemed like all the animals had just had babies. Glossy hens crossed our path followed by a stream of yellow chicks, wide-eyed calves suckled their mothers, crazy kids skipped around long-suffering mother goats and puppies nestled in a sleepy huddle by their mother's teats. Here was Mother Nature at her most alluring, she had painted this picture with her brightest of palettes making sure she washed each brush thoroughly before painting in a new colour. The trees whispered to us as we rode past, "procreate, procreate, here is abundance in all its simplicity".

Unfortunately we still had our band of protectors, our Achilles heel which, although made this possible, was now magnified against the picture of tranquillity. It was like riding to the accompaniment of the sonic boom. We came to a clearing in the woods and were told to stop. It was the end of Baloo's jurisdiction and we had to wait for the new escorts to arrive. No sooner had he said so the new recruits came into view; this was turning out to be a military operation worthy of the Changing of the Guard. Each policemen wanted to say goodbye in turn, especially to Glenna and I. Their eyes appeared glazed with gratification and they bowed their heads as we shook their hands as if honoured to have followed us for eight slow hours. It was hard to get used to.

And so we set off again with our new cast of bodyguards. The afternoon sun was flickering at us through the trees, the last bit of heat turning our legs a soft pink. Relaxed and with no energy to go a metre more we entered the enclosures of the Sanctuary. We fell silent. I had never been anywhere where the presence of animals was so palpable. In this small corner of the world humans took second place. The few houses that there were appeared in a state of severe dilapidation, there was no electricity and no running water. Every rupee put into the park was for the sake of the animals. The atmosphere here was serious, binocular toting tourists were not welcome. The park was inhabited by three species only - the rangers, the poachers and the endangered animals.

It was dusk and we sat on the veranda looking out into the bush, the trees ramrod straight and faultlessly smooth until exploding into a canopy of leaves above us. Behind us we could hear the sounds of our dinner being prepared, the smell of onions and spices agitating our hunger. Tim and I played backgammon with the bamboo pieces. This was as near to perfection as any place on earth. We could even salute it with a bottle of gin; no ice, no slice, no tonic, only its effects coursing through the body to permeate our muscles.

When people speak derisively of prolonged travel, when they use words such as indulgence and escapism, there is a part of me that feels the need to justify. "I am travelling because I am doing research for a PhD" or "I am coming to Assam because my great-grandfather worked in the East India Company". But if one were just to say I'm travelling because I like travelling, that reason could only be used once.

On the next trip people would think you were a bit of a flake, one of life's drop-outs, aimless, a waster even. If travel equates to pleasure then that is not reason enough to travel, the trip must be justified say the dedicated conformists. Well, everything in moderation is my theory.

But an evening such as this, far removed from anything that I have ever known, will stay forever in my memory bank. Sometimes I will choose to withdraw it, rolling it around in my head and reliving every part and then at other times it will resurface unexpectedly, paralysing me mid-task with the intensity of the recollection. If life is a magnum opus then moments like these are the best chapters.

The head ranger popped by just before supper; he wanted to see who the interlopers were in his park. He was pretty surprised to see us, even more so the bicycles, but when we gave him the name of his colleague whom we met in Guwahati he was welcoming and chatty. He told us he had had a bad day, a bad year in fact. He was tired and in desperate need of a miracle. We hurriedly offered him our gin, he declined and continued to chain smoke his beedies.

His problem was with the poachers, there were too many of them and too few rangers to control them. Tiger poaching poses a serious threat to India, one tiger is killed every day and now only three thousand remain. It is a fearfully lucrative business; the tigers are shipped to Hong Kong where their bones are believed to have healing properties, their penises are used for aphrodisiacal purposes (how unoriginal) and their claws and pelts sold for astronomical prices. But in controlling the poachers the situation was getting out of hand, it was turning into a weapons' war. The parks were drastically underfunded and undermanned. Compared to the high powered automatic rifles and German machine guns that the poachers used the rangers were at a gross disadvantage, all they had were old second-hand rifles. These days it wasn't only the tigers getting killed but people too.

Further up the state of Assam in Kaziranga National Park they face similar problems concerning the near extinction of the one-horned rhinoceros. Poachers kill the rhinos solely for their horns; they shoot the body, slice off the horn with a machete and run off with the priceless booty under their arms. The horn is sold whole to Hong Kong, where it is pulverised and then sold to the rest of Asia for its aphrodisiacal powers. One and a half tons of rhinoceros killed just for its horn to give people the horn. Doesn't it make you wonder about the people who buy this stuff? What sexual aerobics are they performing behind closed doors? What's wrong with a bit of erotic fiction or saucy mags that the rest of us make do with if we need some help in the arousal department?

In the early nineties, twenty-eight rhinos were killed by poachers in one year. Now, thanks to a more ruthless approach, the records show that only one was killed last year. The rangers do not hesitate to shoot anyone found off the designated path that circumnavigates Kaziranga. They would be presumed a poacher and therefore shot. Many lives have been lost but there seems to be no other alternative.

'You want to come out on patrol with me tonight?' asked our ranger.

'You bet.'

'OK but I warn you, first I may have to kill a man. You must mentally prepare yourselves.' And with that he got up and left the veranda.

Well, that was an ambiguous statement if ever I heard one. Did he mean that whilst on patrol he might have to kill someone so we should mentally prepare ourselves for that? Or did he mean that first he may have to kill someone but he wouldn't know how long it was going to take so we should mentally prepare ourselves to wait? I had visions of a captive poacher being led to a deserted spot deep in the heart of the Sanctuary. A couple of men hold him down whilst our ranger took up position in front of him. Under the glow of the moon he would pull the trigger shooting him between the eyes, the exact place where the poacher had killed the tiger.

'Your food is ready.' The chowdikkar had slipped in unnoticed whilst we were gawping at each other.

A few hours later, as we were pouring the rest of the gin over a fruit salad, we heard a knock at the door.

'Are you ready?'

The ranger had come for us. It was nearing midnight. We followed him to his jeep trying to catch a glimpse of his face.

'Do you think he's killed him yet?' I whispered to Glenna.

'I don't know. He seems too cheerful.'

'Yeah, well maybe it's cause for celebration; one less poacher to worry about.'

We set off down the track, the beam from the headlights illuminating the bush in front of us. Every so often we would come across small camps or the odd bungalow like ours, he got out taking his rifle with him.

'Maybe this is it. Listen for a gun shot.'

We glued our faces to the windows. Nothing! He came back and off we went again.

Going deeper into the park we noticed the sky ahead lit with an orange glow, the source - a huge bonfire, its flames crackling and spitting into the night sky surrounded by a group of men. We got out of the jeep and our ears were full of the sounds of munching interrupted by snorts and cries. He had brought us to the elephant camp. Chained by their feet to a group of trees were five young elephants tucking into their supper, a mound of leaves and shoots lying at their feet. They were between five and seven years old, still babies and in their second year of training, they had three more years to go. One of them, a young feisty tusker, which we could tell was everyone's favourite, was a troublemaker and the cause of many headaches. Only yesterday he put his trunk through an open window and in an attempt to be friendly tried to duff one of the rangers on the head whilst he was sitting at his desk. I was wary, as soon as the trunk came up I leapt back to safety. The beasts' sonorous cries, their ears pinned to the side of their heads, reverberated deep in our bones. Were they crying for their mums? We were assured that they weren't unhappy.

Our elephant watching over, we went and sat around the fire drinking tea with the men. The desire to sleep was strong. I lay back on one of the bamboo benches and gazed up at the stars trying to put a name to the jungle sounds I was hearing. People try to manufacture this back home; you can buy those fluorescent stars to stick on your ceiling and nature sounds to play on your stereo. It sure doesn't come close to the real thing.

We arrived back at the bungalow to find a raging fire outside the veranda. Just as we were about to panic the ranger told us it was only an elephant deterrent. During the night they come looking for food and can cause severe damage to a house; a fire is a necessity. What a hassle! I tried to think what it must be like incorporating that domestic chore into an already hectic lifestyle.

'Darling – it's your turn to build the fire tonight and make sure you don't leave any gaps, the elephants are getting blasé.'

If such a hazard was commonplace in the western world you could be sure that marketing would take the edge off it. No doubt we would be able to buy month supplies of "Jumbo Repellent Fire Kits" at our local garage along with disposable barbecues and upholstery cleaners.

Well, I didn't see my tiger. They say you're blessed if you do.

Probably lots saw me, I just couldn't see them.

'Tim! I think I've killed the dog.'

That morning I had deposited our fruit salad in the bush at the back of the house. I thought it would be a nice treat for the animals. I had forgotten that we had doused it in gin. I had not considered that one animal would eat the whole thing. The poor creature, who was a rangy, diseased mutt in the first place, did not know what had happened to him. He staggered round the side of the house looking uncertain as to where he was or who he was even. His eyes seemed to look at me beseechingly.

'Woman! What have you done to me? Help. Help'

He managed three more shaky steps, then collapsed to the ground, head resting on his paws in a picture of misery. We had no time to see if he regained consciousness, the escorts had arrived to take us back to Orang.

Retracing our steps through Wonderland, we stopped in front of a gaily coloured tent from which festive music was blaring out. We poked our heads inside whereupon we were immediately taken by the hands and pulled into the bosom of a wedding party. A curious band of old clarinets and tarnished trumpets played an interesting mixture of samba and Hindi rock whilst a young lad and girl danced with abandon in the middle of a circle.

'Go on Poll, join in, show 'em how a pro does it.'

I gave Tim my most withering look. If I had a turkey for every time someone said that to me then I would have a factory to challenge Bernard Matthews. When we go round to friends for dinner I would hardly tell him to go and chop an onion with the cook just so they could see how a pro does it. My father is actually the worst. I spent many school holidays in Indonesia, especially Bali, where they have a repertoire of exotic national dances. The Monkey Dance is especially ritualistic and incorporates mass leaping, tumbling and high-pitched wallering. I remember watching it for the first time glued to my seat feeling both terrified and exhilarated at the same time. I felt a nudge in the ribs, 'Poll, do you think you could do that?'

'No.'

'I bet you could, go and join them.'

'Dad! No way. Ssh.'

'Go on, they would love it.'

'Yeah well I wouldn't.'

'Go up and join the end of the line.'

'Dad stop it! Anyway my fingers don't bend back like theirs.'

Hindu weddings are a lengthy and elaborate occasion. Hours are spent on the preparation not just of the ceremony itself but in the choosing of a suitable partner. Forget meeting your future husband at a friend's dinner party or bumping up against him in a sweaty night-club. Imagine instead your parents signing on to a marriage bureau and most certainly consulting horoscopes to narrow down the search to make sure that the future holds all the right credentials for a successful marriage: children, health, wealth. Note the word successful as opposed to loving. It is different now but in the past couples would not even meet until their wedding day.

The ceremony itself lasts three hours and is laden with rituals and protestations to the auspicious god Ganesh, the pot-bellied, elephant-headed god of wisdom and the remover of obstacles. They say his knowledge is infinite and his judgement just; only good comes from Lord Ganesh. He staves off misfortune and makes sure the timing of events in one's life is purely lead by karma from within. Before any important undertaking he is always worshipped.

Our bride was dressed in a red and gold sari, her hands and feet henna-dyed in intricate patterns. She wore half of Ratners the Jewellers on her wrists and fingers and both she and her husband wore a garland of flowers around their necks. The ceremony was long over and now they were enjoying postnuptial bliss, except that they looked anything but blissful.

In my mind, Hindu marriage vows must be some of the most beautiful words that one could say to someone else. Perhaps it was the solemnity of the words that took the smile from our bride's face.

"I am the sky, you are the earth. I am the melody, you are the hymn.'

But the important part of the ceremony was taking seven steps together to represent walking along life's path as a union. Each step stood for an aspect of their life together, one step for strength, one for wealth, food, children, happiness, friendships and seasons. For Hindus marriage marks the beginning of the second stage of life, the time of being a householder. It is in this stage that one fulfils life's important duties such as having children and supporting family members.

Strict Hindus believe in one life, one husband; marriage should only end when one of them dies. The disgrace to both families should the marriage not work would be too much to bear. Should the husband die then levirate marriages are sometimes allowed. This is when the wife marries her brother-in-law or another close relative mainly to bear a child on behalf of the deceased husband.

A widow is looked upon as an unlucky omen to have at a wedding and, if she is young, is considered sexually threatening. It is therefore common for widows to embark on a spiritual marriage to Krishna, seeking solace in their love for him and alleviating some of the disgrace attached.

We were called into a small annexe and given sweets and delicacies by the parents of the bride. They seemed chuffed to pieces that we had rolled up at their daughter's wedding, we were surely a good omen bringing with us all the fortunes of the western world. Well that was questionable but what we did bring with us was fifteen, hungry, armed guards who were tucking into the wedding fayre with huge enjoyment.

We could have stayed for ages but after a while our guards seemed to be getting restless and made it clear that they wanted us to move on. We said our thank yous and bade farewell but not before distributing some stickers and balloons for the kids. We had not taken into account that our presents were desirable to all generations. We watched in disbelief as a ninety year-old grandfather swiped a balloon from his grandson's hands and clutched it to his chest in a toothless grin, paying no heed whatsoever to the tears of protest that followed. So much for selfless grandfatherly love, if my grandfather did that I would have boycotted his knee forever.

As we rode on we noticed something was missing. No one said anything, we didn't want to spoil the moment for we believed it to be short-lived. We waited and waited but still it didn't come. For some reason our escort was no longer following us. We were cycling in paradise with nothing but the sound of the gravel flicking from underneath our tyres, the odd jangle of our bells as we bumped over a stone and the clip-clopping of cows ambling along the path. It was too balmy, too gentle on the senses to be ruined by militant unrest, surely they wouldn't hang out here? It was impossible for criminal activity to flourish amongst such bewitching charm. Brahmin knew that he had created a slice of perfection and he was going to make sure it remained that way, I had no doubt.

I was right, we made it back to Orang still alone and still alive. Superintendent N.R. Roy At Your Every Service greeted us with alarm when he saw that we were unaccompanied. He began a Saint Vitus dance of agitation.

'I am not understanding. Please to be excusing, this is very very bad, very very bad.'

An hour and a half later the boys showed up, towed behind a TaTa truck, looking more sheepish then a flock ready for shearing. They had broken down and had to wait for a passing truck to tow them back to Orang. But according to N.R. Roy At Your Every Service he had told the mechanic to fix the engine last week which very apparently he never did.

'Dearie me. So many peoples not doing their jobs properly. *Acha, acha.* I told him to fix it but he is too lazy. I shall have to be punishing him severely for this. It is very very bad. If the District Commissioner hears of this incompetence then I will be losing my job.'

Uh Oh! We did feel bad. Here we were getting people in trouble, perhaps making people lose their jobs. This was not turning out how we wanted at all.

We were taken by convoy to the Inspection Bungalow and left alone for all of two minutes until a knock on the door heralded the arrival of a bunch of school kids and their teacher. We duly signed the autograph books and dished out stickers.

About to embark on a knicker washing spree so I would have something to wear tomorrow for the next batch of police guards, the door opened again and our room was filled with rustling saris and reams of glossy hair. The wives and the sisters-in-law and the aunts and the great aunts of the officers of the police station had come to pay us a visit. I have no doubt that they were charming ladies but they proved damned hard work to entertain. They sat squished together on the sofa and stuck to the back of the wall, faces expressionless. Only their eyes gave any sign of life as they travelled from Glenna's head to mine (yes, we know we will never find Indian husbands), over our chests, taking an avid interest in the shape of our legs under our trousers, then down to our feet where we could hear sharp intakes of breath. What? What's wrong with us now? Our shoes! Or the cause of their distress, our sandals. Women of the higher castes would never show their feet in public no matter how hot it was. We looked at their feet. Without exception each pair was stuffed into chaste little court shoes. This flummoxed the lovely ladies, etiquette was now thrown into confusion. Who should be paying respects to who?

Thankfully the next band of visitors arrived and the ladies took this as their excuse to leave and bustled out of the door, expectation thrown into disarray. Now standing before us were the local businessmen, the big swinging dicks around town. They were a smooth bunch who I don't think were bothered by our sandals. They made us promise to visit each of their establishments in the morning; let's see, that was one chemist, three doctors and four shops. That would be eight cups of tea before we had even cycled a kilometre. Before leaving they got out their autograph books as well. The shopkeeper who stocked the books must have made a killing that evening as each book we had written in that night was brand spanking new.

At last peace and quiet. The strain of having to make conversation was beginning to become a chore, all we wanted was to eat and relax and sprawl our bodies over the furniture. This was not to be, N.R. Roy At Your Every Service appeared with brother-in-law in tow and a bottle of whisky in hand. I never drink whisky but one can't be fussy in the outback of Assam. For defence whisky it was very drinkable and we all became merry apart from N.R. Roy At Your Every Service who got plastered. Dinner arrived cooked by his wife.

'My wife very very pretty and very very fatty.'

We saw her the next day and felt that N.R. Roy should put negatives in front of each of his descriptions. Although ample of flesh, she was not grossly fat; however, not even under the influence of a mind-altering love drug could our host's wife ever be described as pretty; let's just say moose woman and leave it at that. What she lacked in features she made up for in culinary prowess, she was a most sublime cook. We did not stop eating for a good couple of hours. Bowl after bowl of delicious curries and *dhals* were placed before us, each dish subtly different from the last, her knowledge and use of spices so utterly perfect.

Of all the senses taste is the only one which brings on involuntary groans long after the first instant has passed. I have never been rendered speechless for such a long period of time, unable to make any coherent sounds other than moans of pleasure. That was it, my curries down at Raj of India on Chiswick High Road ruined forever now that I had eaten Indian food like this. Another bottle of whisky came out.

'Just to be having one more before I go on duty.'

One more glass or one more bottle? It turned out to be one more bottle and one more packet of fags, but at least the mosquitoes were absent. His duty started at 11.00 pm and finished at 3.00 or 4.00 am depending on what trouble with the militants was brewing that night. He started again at 7.00 the following morning.

'N.R. Roy, it is essential for you officers to drink I think?'

'Most essential, very essential. Our job's too hard.'

We just wanted to see if the consensus was the same throughout northeast India as regards to alcoholism and defence personnel booze. He got up to leave, wobbling, and kissed us all passionately on our hands.

'I love you! You all very special to me. Please it would be big honour for me if you came for breakfast in my house tomorrow.'

He told us not to worry for our safety, he had the Inspection Bungalow surrounded by guards, no one would be allowed in who wasn't personally vetted by him. The Bodo extremists, he warned, come in the guise of normal friendly people, trust no one. Well it was a bit late in the day for those words of comfort seeing as we had already held court to half the population of the town already.

Before going to bed I poked my nose outside the door. Sure enough there were the sentinels keeping vigil outside the house. I shook my head, sometimes I felt like I was in 'Carry On Up The Brahmaputra'.

17

THE BOREDOM OF BIRDWATCHING

Dattatreya was born as the three incarnations of Brahma, Siva and Vishnu. When they were young their father went to embrace all of them whereupon they amalgamated into one upon his touch. The knowledge and power from each individual was now combined into one. Dattatreya taught his doctrine of self-realisation through his gentle and loving character.

> *The Earth taught me patience and generosity.*
> *The Ocean taught me to remain the same in spite of storms.*
> *The Fire taught me to give myself so that I would shine brightly.*
> *The Air taught me to move freely anywhere and not to stay in one place.*
> *The Water taught me how much purity is needed for good health.*
> *The Sky taught me to be above everything and yet embrace all things.*
> *The Moon taught me that the self remains the same even when appearance changes.*
> *The Sun taught me that a luminous face is reflected by all smooth surfaces.*
> *The Dove taught me that love means feeding one's own family.*
> *The Bee taught me to collect sweet wisdom from places where no one suspected it to be.*

The Arrow-maker taught me to be purposeful and
always concentrated on one point.
The Snake taught me to be content to live in a hole or
cave and build no house.
The Fish taught me never to take the bait and so
destroy myself.
The Owl taught me to sit peacefully and be content
with little food.

N.R. Roy and his family, although N.R. Roy's participation is perhaps more sporadic, rise at dawn every day. Before they speak to anyone they utter the name of their chosen deity - Dattatreya. Having spoken his name they then look to the palms of their hands so that the first thing they behold is an auspicious object. This done they go outside and touch the earth, in doing so performing an auspicious action. In the corner of their house is the shrine, the focal point of their daily worship, a brightly coloured corner decorated with images of their deity and surrounded by flowers and incense.

It is here that they perform *Puja*, which means worship, consisting of rituals that use all of the five senses thus ensuring that the person is fully present. A bell is rung, the god washed and dressed and offered food which then becomes sacred. They light a lamp and burn the incense and then recite prayers; on odd occasions they also read some of the scriptures out of the sacred books. They finish their worship by eating the sacred food (*prashad*) and thinking about the day ahead and how to increase *dharma,* righteousness, and *artha* which means wealth.

Hindus believe that they are born with debts to pay - debts to the deities, the sages, teachers and parents, humankind and all living beings. The deities can be appeased by daily worship, the sages satisfied by studying the scriptures, teachers and parents placated by gifts, humankind honoured by being given food if they were to ask and all living beings acknowledged by giving the leftovers from the daily meal to the animals.

N.R. Roy and Mrs Fatty and Pretty were paying off their debts to humankind tenfold that day. Again we tasted ambrosia from the hands of N.R. Roy's wife, she had most certainly done her husband proud. Their tiny, spotless house was chock full with a succession of inquisitors dressed in their best saris and smartest shirts. N.R. Roy took charge of the photo session positioning us on the bed along with the chosen few. But what to do to get them to smile?

'*Paneer*!' We tried hopefully.

Not even a glimmer. Nothing. This was far too important an occasion, their smiling countenances were replaced with grave expressions more fitting to a parliamentary line-up than a happy snappy photo.

When it was time to leave the whole of the village turned out to say goodbye. The mechanic had still not done his job, so in place of the jeep we now had a cumbersome truck plus a stately Ambassador car housing N.R Roy and a few of the other higher officers. We cycled to the border of the next district and stopped. N.R Roy hopped out to give us heartfelt goodbyes and a bottle of defence whisky. He had tears in his eyes and his voice was wracked with emotion. We promised we would write. Farewell Orang, you were an experience never to forget.

Lee had had enough, he dismissed our escorts at the next tea stop. They looked nervous. I felt it. They obviously didn't think this such a good idea and adopted another tactic, racing on ahead then waiting for us to appear, then continuing on and so forth. I liked this set-up, this way we had the best of both worlds, cycling in peace yet with peace of mind. Lee didn't, at the next stop he told them they weren't needed.

Alone and unprotected we carried on. There was an army presence everywhere which I didn't know whether to take as comforting or not. We stopped for lunch at a roadside shack and were approached by three men. They started with the usual questions: where were we from? Where were we going?

'At what time you reaching Eco Camp?'

Hang on a minute, wasn't that a little more information than they needed to know? We all became instantly suspicious and evaded the question. Thank God that we were not doing the typical 'India trip' and taking every amphetamine and barbiturate known to man, we were paranoid enough without extra delusive fears of our own making. The guys picked up on the vibes.

'Please not to be worrying, no reason, only to be curious.'

We continued on. It was 3.00pm February 12th 1999. I was in Assam, not a wise place to be, wishing with all my might that I was anywhere but where I was. The insides of my thighs stung from sweat and the rubbing of my shorts against the saddle. My back was on the brink of spasm, jarred from hours of bumping along rotten roads. My hands were covered in blisters, I had lost my cycling gloves somewhere along the route and the tape on my handlebars had rubbed away my skin. My knees felt like they belonged to someone else and the flesh that came in contact with the saddle was covered in friction spots. The cycling was not enjoyable as I was too fearful for my safety and I cursed each kilometre until arriving at the destination.

I was doing this for love. Was I stupid? Did I not have a life of my own? Was I one of those women who followed their men blindly wherever they went, whatever they did? If Tim were to start playing golf would I also buy a Pringle sweater and become a member of a golf club? Did it mean that I didn't value my life as much as his? Did it mean that I wanted to please him or was it that I thought Tim enjoyed life much more than me and I wanted a piece of it too? To what other extents would I go? What was moving to New Zealand if not a huge personal surrender to this thing we call love.

'Tim, if I were to travel through every country in Europe learning their national dances would you come with me?'

'Yes.' Amazingly he didn't hesitate. 'I might not actually participate in the dancing but I would come with you and document it differently. Why?'

'I'm just wondering how much people would forget their own immediate lives in order to do something solely for love.'

'If I wanted to skateboard around Iran would you come with me?'

'NO!' I didn't hesitate either.

'Phew! There you go, it shows that actually you still do what you want to do. It's important to embrace new things and put yourself in situations that you would never normally do, but to keep your identity you also have to know when to say "Baby, you're doing this alone." '

I had made up my mind what I was going to do. There was no doubt in my head as to how much I loved Tim. He was the person I most enjoyed being with, time spent with him was not a minute wasted. He inspired me, challenged me, soothed me and exacerbated me. With him I had no limitations, no criteria to fit. His love was huge and warm and generous and what's more he loved being loved by me too. A future without him seemed desolate and lonely. He rocked my world.

But I am a cautious person. A previous boyfriend used to call me his "But Girl" unfortunately not referring to my bum. It is true many of my sentences start with that little word, accompanied by a puckering between the eyebrows and consternation in the voice. I believe everything must be taken into account before a decision is made, every avenue explored and each 'but' placated. In terms of the New Zealand issue I had quite a few. We had survived the test of India *but* could we survive the test of being separated? I thought our love solid *but* could it stand up to temptation when we would be so far apart? I thought I knew that Tim was the one *but* what if I didn't miss him as much as I thought? What if he met someone else? What if I didn't mind that much?

So my decision was to go to New Zealand but not before a good few months spent apart. Here I was putting another test to our love but I wanted to know for sure where we really stood. I sincerely hoped that one day I would give up this need for guarantees because deep down I knew that there were none. Time spent together, time spent apart, time spent in horrible circumstances, times spent in paradise, that is still not to say that we could live happily ever after. If only choosing a mate was as simple as completing a workbook full of exercises. At the end the marks from each exercise would be toted up and fall into one of three categories:

Outcome A: No more than 10 points scored.

Forget it.

Outcome B: Between 10 and 20 points scored.

Worth a go but could ultimately lead to animosity, marriage guidance counselling and bitterness.

Outcome C: Between 20 and 30 points scored.

This is as good as it gets, dispel any ideas of grandeur and grab it whilst you can.

At least then you would definitely know. If you scored twenty-six you knew not to waste another minute of your time fantasising about how life would be if you were dating the chap in Corporate Finance or the girl with the sexy eyes in your swimming sessions. Similarly, when the dulcet tones of your Yoga teacher makes you lose all conscious reasoning you could complete the exercises in the workbook and bring yourself back to reality by finding out that actually you and Mr. Beefcake (or Soyacake) only scored a measly four. Sadly they don't exist but I was going to try my damnedest to make up my own set of foolproof exercises anyway.

If the choicest fruits are found on the furthest branches then the Eco Camp in Potasali Wildlife Park had to be the sweetest lychee of them all. Whether places like this seemed all the more spectacular for the sheer fact that our legs had peddled us there I do not know. As we struck off the main road we took a track leading into the jungle. Similar to the track to Orang Wildlife Sanctuary the strains of impending danger seemed to gradually dissipate and my heartbeat slowed down. We cycled round a corner and the gates to the camp came into view. All my earlier negative thoughts and my hatred of this cycle touring nonsense slipped away. We had arrived in paradise once again.

The camp was a grassy clearing in the middle of the jungle decked out with old-fashioned, circus-style tents each covered with a thatch roof, the eaves providing a shelter to sit under. In the distance we could hear the running water of the Potasali River swollen with ice melt from the Himalayas. This was a camp for the elite, the wealthy Assamese came here to fish and to spend the weekend relaxing and game watching. At last we felt like we could relax, we could be sure that no one wanted our autographs here.

S.P. was the manager of the camp. He was a gentle and erudite man who had a different slant on the troubles of his state. In his opinion we were perfectly safe, the Bodo extremists would never harm children or tourists. They did not, after all, want to appear total barbarians otherwise the government would never give them control of their own state. He thought that the District Commissioner had been wrong to give us such an extensive escort, it was only attracting attention to us.

With all the pomp and ceremony the extremists might have thought we were more important than we were, another lucrative group of people to bump off other than innocent tourists. Part of me had considered that too. By all accounts our escort days were over in any case. In two days time we were to cross the Brahmaputra River to the southern part of the state, where all was supposedly peaceful.

The following morning we were woken whilst it was still dark and taken to the edge of the Potasali River. As the sun slowly began to rise we saw a shadowy figure punt his way across the water towards us. We stepped into the dugout and crossed to the other side, the sun a low skimming ball bouncing off the water's edge. We pulled the boat up the shingle beach and set off into the jungle down swampy paths, past bubbling rivers, across dried out riverbeds and into the heart of the jungle.

We followed behind the warden in single file who hopped over fallen branches and dipped under fronds as if not burdened by joints and tendons like the rest of humanity. His body seemed to be drenched with olive oil, seamless, fluid, graceful. I don't know if I was more mesmerised by him or the abundance that dripped with overproductivity, here the Green Revolution had most certainly won. This jungle was prodigal and riotous, monkeys leapt from tree to tree and birds and butterflies littered the sky. Our warden was the Pavarotti of animal noises, his ululation rang out clear and tuneful whilst we stood holding our breath, waiting for answers.

I have a confession – I have no time for birdwatching. I have tried in my past to get excited but I can't. To me birdwatching means dull, dull, dull. I appreciate that to ornithologists it must appear that I have a desperate flaw in my character. For me birdwatching is on a par with neckache, eyestrain, frustration and tedium. A red-breasted hornbill was spotted perched high in a tree. The binoculars came out.

If one person gets a clear picture from the binoculars there is no guarantee that the next person will. When it came to my turn I could have been looking at anything that was green. Looking at trees through binoculars is like doing one of those conceptual tests called 'Magic Eye'. To the uninitiated or the conceptually challenged it appears to be one page of minute dots. If however you were to alternate between squinting and gazing then a picture, so I am told, emerges clearly. It took a good while to bring the tree into focus, to work out what was the branch and what was the warden's leg.

'Left a bit, right a bit, lift the binoculars higher. No, no, not that high.'

Oh Jesus! And then the bloody bird flew off anyway. No, it is not a pastime for me.

I was punished for having these thoughts. As I stood under the tree waiting for the others to track down the errant red-breasted hornbill a red blob grazed my arm and landed with a splotch on my foot. Obviously I was being reprimanded for my un-politically correct thoughts by a menstruating monkey. Either that or betel nut is not enjoyed solely by humans.

We walked for three hours following tiger footprints but the beast remained elusive. Instead we saw lone elephant tuskers, a herd of water buffalo and, at the cattle camp, the debris of the outhouses that an elephant had destroyed the night before. It could have been a twister that rampaged the camp for all the damage that was caused, but we were told it was the work of just one elephant.

Back at Eco Camp the pace was slow and melodic. I will always remember India for its music, not the Hindustani religious music or the *sitar* and *tabla*, or even the Hindi rock that seemed to accompany us everywhere, but the music of rural Indian life. I sat in my deckchair under the eaves of our tent; I didn't want to read or talk I just wanted to listen. The sound of women's voices as they sat in a clump on the grass talking softly and rapidly was as beautiful and lilting as a song.

Women talking en masse only sound beautiful when you can't understand what they are saying, when you can't tune in to the bitching and the gossiping or the harshness of swearing. It is the allure of incomprehension that rewards the ears, the rises and falls, crescendos and syncopation, this is what turns conversation into symphonies. When at home do we have the chance to listen to the rasping, rhythmic sound of a twig brush or the clanking of pots and pans without the adulteration of an urban hum, or the more intrusive sirens and screeching brakes, aeroplanes and blaring music?

I sometimes become obsessed with noises, it is my indication to how wound up I am. When I worked for a while in Tokyo I felt physical pain through my chest when I lay in bed at night. My room looked out over an intersection of one of the many flyovers. Lorries whistled past my window throughout the course of the night and the sound of them bumping over the metal grids went straight through me like a lance. I would wake in the morning with a tenderness in my chest.

I know when I am stressed in London by the amount of attention I pay to the electrical hums in my room. If you don't listen for them they are imperceptible but if you concentrate enough then just the hum of the stereo on standby can be deafening to me. I sometimes have to get up in the middle of the night and switch off all the plugs. But the sounds are still there. I go and stick my head out of the window thinking that perhaps it is the sound of the street lamps. It *is* the sound of the street lamps but not just in Cranbrook Road, but in Knightsbridge and Clapham Common and the whole of Greater London. The mass load of electrical currents that surge around the city vibrating with an energy that I am powerless to switch off and which in turn sends a current of energy through my veins. The noises make me restless.

But not here. I listened and listened but there were no electrical hums, only the sounds of human and animal life living simply. I did not want to spoil it with stimulation of any other kind.

'Poll, will you cut my hair?' Tim asked.

'Later, I'm listening.'

We left the camp the following afternoon heading for the town of Tezpur. We had to retrace our steps for part of the journey and found ourselves stopping at the same food inn as we had on our way out. The owner thought that we had been sent from the heavens. Between us we ate enough to keep him financially afloat for a week. A fan was pulled out from a dark corner, special tomato and onion *raita* was added as an extra to our *samosas*, we were given special sweets and the freshest tea.

Absolutely everything was the same as two days before. The man sitting on his *paan* cart sat in the same crossed-legged position, his hand darting into the separate containers picking a bit of this and a bit of that for the betel nut cocktail. It was the same little girl, perhaps his granddaughter, still in the same yellow, flouncy dress perched opposite him, not doing anything specific but staring at us with her head cocked to one side just as she did two days ago. If we were to come back in one year's time would things still be the same? I found it stultifying and depressing and wanted to leave as soon as we had finished. The owner shouted after us, 'Goodbye, you come tomorrow?' I'm afraid not, time is running out.

Tezpur sits on the northern banks of the Brahmaputra. The river is so wide that you cannot see the other side. We walked up to Agnigarh Hill to watch the sunset. The tide was low leaving asymmetrical islands that broke up the vast expanse of water. There were a few fishing boats out, silhouetted black in the fading light. The air was thick with midges and mosquitoes. It was a moody, tropical scene that intoxicated and alienated me at the same time.

Travelling is a curious thing, just when you think you have it down to a T a cloud passes over the sun making you feel a tentative, intimidated novice all over again. Just when I thought I had cast all apprehension aside, when I thought I had become used to the nomadic existence, the daily rape of my senses, the acceptance of the bizarre and the exotic, a change of light was all it took to make me feel like the floor had been taken from under me. Travelling accentuated whatever mood I was in; if I was light spirited then it made me ecstatic, if I was vulnerable then it made me feel useless and if I was lonely then I felt bereft. Tim and I had four more nights together – until now I felt obvious anticipation but as the shadows lengthened on the Brahmaputra and the first of the lanterns on the fishing boats were lit all I felt was dread.

But travel does not let you indulge for long, there is always a list of objectives to be dealt with. The most pressing one for us was where to stay that night. We followed our usual procedure of going to the police station but it was Sunday night, the town was celebrating a festival and there was a serious fire. The officer in charge was in the middle of trying to enlist the fire engines from the neighbouring district to help. Either the phone line was not working efficiently or the guy on the other end couldn't understand the officer's English. For an emergency service procedures weren't running smoothly.

'HELLO – HELLO – HELLO WE NEED YOUR HELP – HELLO – HELLO – HELLO, WE HAVE A FIRE – HELLO – HELLO – HELP – PLEASE SEND – HELLO – HELLO.'

We stood around the table trying not to look amused as the number of casualties rose alarmingly. We decided we might have better luck with the locals.

Indians, instead of saying, 'I don't know', will point you in any direction rather than appear unhelpful. Endearing? Infuriating! We spent a long hour being sent in circles. We spent an even longer hour shouting at each other. We came across one lad twice; we pounced on him.

'Which way to the Inspection Bungalow please?'

'At the end of the road please to be turning right.'

'But last time you said turn left.'

'Yes.'

'We didn't find it. Which way you think this time?'

'Yes.'

'What yes? Right or left?'

He scratched his eyebrow.

'Right?'

He nodded.

'Or left?'

He nodded.

'You don't know do you?'

His eyes turned sheepish and his head started on the figure of eight. Hah! Now we knew where we stood, he hadn't the faintest idea.

Tim is a vegetarian who does not believe in killing anything, not a cow, nor a fly and most definitely not an ant. He believes that he is not justified to make a decision on another creature's life especially when he doesn't see the need to eat meat in order to survive. If he were to kill something then he would do so with the full understanding that one day, or one lifetime, he would have to accept the consequences that would rebound on him, in other words karma.

Karma - that hazy word that now has become commonplace in modern vocabulary. Good karma and bad karma are phrases bandied around bringing a snarl to the cynics and a pious glow to the righteous.

Apparently there is no such thing as good or bad karma, it is the universal principle of cause and effect, action and reaction which governs all life. Harsh karma only means an experience that helps us to grow, often bringing with it the slap round the face to spiritual transformation. Karma should be the natural law of the mind, as straightforward as gravity being the law of matter. The principle is simple. Good and loving actions bring to us love and kindness, evil and selfish actions bring to us pain and suffering.

"According as one acts, so does he become. One becomes virtuous by virtuous action, bad by bad action."

Our future is determined by the karma we have incurred through our thoughts, words and deeds not only in this life but in our previous lives as well.

Well I was stuffed! I can't actually remember what I was like in my past lives but if this one is anything to go by then I have a future of pain and suffering awaiting me. Why, oh why, did I spend a summer vacuuming up ants from an ant nest that had taken up residence in the skirting board of my patio doors? I annihilated hundreds at a time; poor innocent souls sucked into the abyss of Henry the vacuum cleaner. What about all the mosquitoes I have splattered against white walls, their innards encrusted there for posterity. I wonder if perhaps the divine law makes a concession for mosquitoes seeing as they bring no worldly benefit whatsoever. I used to blow smoke into the ears of my friend's kitten to make him sneeze, my favourite meal is steak tartar, and I littered a house with mousetraps. Was it too late? If I changed my ways now could the damage be reversed?

There is something to be said for the laws of karma, perhaps it isn't for nothing that I call Tim 'golden balls.' He is the luckiest person I know, things seem to come to him via the most direct route. He never seems to thrash about in fits of indecision or have to deal with disappointment as often as I do. What he wants he seems to get. Could it be down to the fact that he refrains from killing?

Right! From that moment on I was not going to kill – directly. I would let the mosquitoes live, I would let the ants run rampant through my sitting room, spiders and flies I would put outside. But as for giving up meat, that would be a hard one. I felt a vegetarian by default in any case but I don't know if I could give up roast lamb entirely, especially if I was going to visit the land of ovine pleasure. It just wouldn't make sense, would it?

My new doctrines were put to the test almost immediately. Our room at the Inspection Bungalow was a mosquito fest again. My book, or its schizophrenic alter ego – my thwacking, squishing, stunning killer machine – lay on the dressing table looking like butter wouldn't melt in its mouth despite its jacket stained with wall-kill. Instead I lit a coil as a deterrent and eyeballed the pests, trying to find equanimity towards them.

To Tim, you see, an ant isn't a tiny, inconsequential, black thing that hangs around sugar. It has come from the nest to do a job such as carrying a crumb the size of four surf boards back to the queen, fulfilling his part in maintaining the smooth running of the colony. He probably has a girlfriend, a little arthropod beauty, all budding thorax and three pairs of shapely legs. Having listened to Tim talk in this way how could I bring myself to kill anything even if he wasn't looking? Forget the altruistic reasons of karma and future lives, every bug I looked at now had a valid life of its own. I knew the importance of eating and I was not going to become possessive over a few crumbs if it meant food for the colonies.

I was surprised how quickly word of our arrival got round in a sizeable town such as Tezpur. Later that evening we went to eat some street food at the festival. As we passed the shacks and houses on our way we heard the conversation interrupted by recognisable words.

'Bicycle!'

And quite often, 'Newzi Land.'

Unfortunately the excitement of the festival, a Hindu festival celebrating the God of Snakes representing all that is good, coupled with the excitement of having westerners in their midst proved too hard to contain. Things got rather messy. We had just enjoyed a most delicious snack– *aloo chat* – potato cakes fried with green peas, tomato salsa, red onion, crushed *puri* and a mixture of sprinkled spices. We were standing in a gathering around the stall, music was blaring, the streets were packed with people, we were shoved and jostled and harangued. Yeah, well we were in India, tell me something new. But there was one group of young lads who were trying everything in their power to get our attention. Having attempted every trick in the book they came up with the idea of charging through us throwing stones at us to get a reaction. On their second charge one of the stones hit Glenna in the face. Understandably she went mad. She shouted, the minxes ran off and the already jammed streets erupted into mayhem. Lee went after them shouting, 'Too much fever! Too much fever!' The reputable men of the town came to us begging, 'Please no mind. No problem. No problem. Come enjoy the festival.'

But it was too late, the giddy atmosphere had somehow turned menacing and we felt we did not have the energy to endure the attention any longer. As luck would have it the policemen materialised out of nowhere and bundled us into motor rickshaws escorting us right up to the gates of the Inspection Bungalow. We were back to VIP treatment once again, but what was more disturbing was that I found myself enjoying it.

"Lips that taste of tears are the best for kissing."

Dorothy Parker

18

'GOODBYE MY DARLING'

Whether by bus, car or boat, no other journey I have ever taken has been so rich in local interaction as cycling through remote India. My existence became more subtle; the changing light meant more to me, the quality of the air, the gradient of the hill, the heat of the sun, the bite of the wind. I felt attached to this small corner of the world, I was it and it was me, we were somehow indistinguishable. This was to be our last day of cycling, that night we would be at Wildgrass, a hotel on the edge of Kaziranga National Park.

We crossed the Brahmaputra, which looked much the same at dawn as it did at dusk - monochrome. We were caught up by two boy racers perched on the same bike on their way to school. They were an ingenious team; the lad at the back peddled and read a magazine, the other steered. After some time they swapped. They had long passed the turn-off for their school but they were having too much of a good time racing us to bother about the unnecessary kilometres they were covering. Tim and the two boys were neck and neck, they were not going to give in and hammed up the occasion by feigning exhaustion and fake heart attacks.

'Heh! Are you going to race us all the way to Kaziranga?' Tim asked.

'It is not possible, sir. I must go to school or my mother will be killing me in my body!'

Shortly afterwards they turned round. It was good to see that the mother figure still wields the hand that punishes.

My back finally went. It seized up so that I could barely bend down or turn from side to side, it had suffered one bump too many. I had nearly made my destination but not quite, I had to resort to a bus ride for the rest of the distance to Kaziranga. I made sure I did not feel a failure by placating myself that we hadn't cycled the entire way anyway. If we had then I would have finished it differently.

The bus dropped Tim and me off in the village and we rode the last few kilometres to the Wildgrass Hotel.

If anyone ever finds themselves in the north-east of India, Guwahati to be exact, then they should give themselves a present. They should not hesitate, deviate or prevaricate but get immediately onto Highway 37 heading towards Jorhat for the life enhancing experience of staying at the Wildgrass Hotel. If there is anyone who wants to do something drastic like jack in their stressful executive job to become a painter of sunsets then they should also get onto Highway 37 towards Jorhat. Likewise if there is anyone who has slumped into such a deep depression that getting up in the morning is an impossibility then come along too, get yourself to Guwahati and onto Highway 37 as well.

But don't go as far as Jorhat. Leave the smog of Guwahati, pass the tea gardens and the banana plantations, stop in the village of Sonarihola and make sure to take the time to talk to the wizened old man who always sits in the Fooding hotel next to the bus stop, spouting truths over his glass of tea. Carry on until the plantations give out to the flat plains of Kaziranga, you may even see a herd of elephants on the horizon. On your left there will be a dirt track heading in towards the park with a brightly painted sign above:

WELCOME TO KAZIRANGA NATIONAL PARK
HOME TO THE ONE-HORNED RHINOCEROS

Ignore it – you can go there in the morning. Now start counting the kilometres in your head, once you have got to five turn right down a sandy path which looks like it is leading into the back of beyond. Dusty kids will run out to greet you, often naked, sometimes in frilly dresses, always with matted hair. Follow the path for a further kilometre, pass an enclave of neat, mud houses until you see dusky pink bricks peeping through the foliage. Quicken your pace, you are nearly there. The gates are always open, enter and walk through the flowering archway to the main house. Welcome to Wildgrass; only remember one thing - don't tell too many people about it.

Wildgrass is imbued with a sense of timelessness, completely confident about its place in this world. It has no ideas of pretence – come here and enjoy its beauty is all that it asks. You will find yourself wanting to kick off your shoes and pad around the gardens touching the rare trees and stroking the velvety petals of the orchids. Mealtimes are big occasions, served in a large, airy dining-room with old-fashioned fans whirring above. Pre-dinner drinks are served outside by the bonfire as the tea planters entertain with traditional dances. Even the Kirov could not assimilate a more perfect corps de ballet.

Tim and I were given our own cottage, tucked away in the corner of the grounds. A white picket fence divided our garden from the creek and wild-flowering meadow beyond. Inside, the walls were hung with paintings of animals and, for the first time since we had arrived in the subcontinent, there was not a striplight in sight.

Amongst this beauty and unassuming charm wandered a man perhaps nearly as beautiful and charming as the place he managed. I said wandered, I should have said minced. Not to break with tradition he was also called by his initials – J.D. – and in keeping with his contemporaries also seemed to possess a few of the same genes as James Brown. Smooth and oiled and dressed in Calvin Klein jeans and a silky close-fitting shirt, his favourite pastime was telling stories which he embellished with theatrical chain-smoking. He had sparkling eyes that Glenna and I noticed were permanently fixed on Lee and Tim.

J.D. came from a wealthy Assamese family. At a young age he

was sent to boarding school in Delhi. By the time he was sixteen there was no trace of the naive country bumpkin from the rural north-east. Education had a lot to do with his transformation but not entirely. It was the seventies and *Saturday Night Fever* was topping the charts. From the moment he first heard the Gibb brothers begin Jive Talking he was hooked, Disco consumed his every waking moment. He spent hours in his room practicing the gyrations of John Travolta; at night he slunk out of the school grounds to go to the discos in downtown New Delhi. He spent all of his pocket money on white jeans and disco albums.

A natural leader and with a charisma to match he gathered together a cast (of sorts) and put on the Indian equivalent to *Saturday Night Fever*, with himself cast, of course, as Tony. His father heard of this venture, was appalled and immediately sent him to the more studious city of Bombay to university. After graduating he travelled the world doing a variety of jobs always looking for something as all consuming as his first love – disco. He fell upon Wildgrass by mistake. He came for a holiday, didn't want to leave, got a job taking visitors into the park and now presides over the establishment like a queen bee welcoming each guest into his life and, although it isn't, it feels like into his home as well.

'But back to organising your time here' said J.D. with a clap of the hands and popping another cigarette into his mouth.

'I am thinking we will wake you at dawn and drive you into the park where you can ride elephants and see the rhinos as the sun rises. Back here for lunch, then to the bird sanctuary (uh oh!) and then for a jeep ride around the park in the afternoon.' Another clap of the hands.

'And then some dancing followed by dinner – we're going to have so much fun. Come on Lee and Tim, let me show you my private house.'

And some of your hip gyrations as well no doubt.

He was right, we had a fantastic time. We sat on one very portly tusker in the early morning following a band of others, each with an Indian family atop. Amongst the legs stumbled three babies who might as well have been hired from a cartoon, every now and then tripping up in the large grooves left by their parents. We went right to the middle of the swampy plains to find the one-horned rhinos. We were magnificently rewarded with a large herd having their breakfast. They were enormous, their skin like pre-historic armour plating with an extra tunic for going into battle. When they turned to face us however, it seemed that God had put a touch of humour into their creation. Perched either side of their spectacular horn (phnarr, phnarr) sat little ears more fitting on a piglet then a mighty beast. These, coupled with tiny beady eyes, made them look a bit thick and very comical. But we knew they were anything but sweet. Tim nearly found out just what they were capable of doing later that day.

That afternoon, just as J.D. had said, we were taken back into the park this time being driven around its entirety by jeep. On board we had a driver, a ranger and an interpreter from Wildgrass, a very eager young man called Sunil who fell madly in love with Glenna's alabaster skin and flaming hair. It was a great drive. We drove through jungle coming out into the plains and came upon a watering hole where a herd of wild elephants were bathing. It was the type of scene that you dream of seeing and that you dream of photographing, especially if you're Tim. We got out of the jeep and stood on the track but we were just that bit too far away to take a photo. Tim asked if he could walk down a little path branching off from the track to get in closer. They allowed us but not further than a designated tree. Tim led the way, followed by the ranger, Lee, me then Glenna. By chance Tim happened to look to his left. He froze for a second then whizzed round hissing 'Rhino!' very fiercely.

Tim had happened upon a lone rhino having a quiet munch hidden amongst the tall grasses. It was eight foot away. We all froze on the spot looking at the ranger whose face had gone white. He pointed to the jeep with the butt of his rifle. We needed no more encouragement and began a John Cleese type dash back to the safety of the jeep, our hearts beating wildly.

Rhinos have notoriously bad eyesight and even at eight foot away it may have been that he couldn't see Tim. To make up for their myopia though their sense of smell is acute. We were lucky it was not downwind otherwise Tim and maybe more of us would have made a more substantial snack than grasses. Tim was rather quiet for the next hour sticking closely to the ranger on further photo expeditions. I put my hand to his heart, it was beating rather faster than normal.

'I knew I would have been fine, the rhino smelt I was a vegetarian. Animal karma, you know what I'm saying!'

'Pah! Give me a break!'

A cloud passed over Wildgrass that evening. The cloud of leaving and the thought of what lay ahead. I thought I had been quite good in not ruining these idyllic last days but the sleepless nights reminded me that something was amiss. Tim and I got up early the following morning and went for a walk down by the creek and through the enclave of huts. A local man on his way to work in the fields fashioned me a walking stick from an over-hanging branch.

Tim and I didn't know what to say to one another. Instead we walked and we walked. We were on different ends of the 'sadness stick', Tim and I. My end was a dense, muddy brown of sadness whereas at Tim's end some of the bark had been pulled away leaving shining, creamy pulp underneath. He was sad of course, but also excited; he was going home after four long years away. He was going to see his family and friends and start a new life there all over again. He started to tell me what we would do when I arrived.

'Ssh Tim. Don't talk like this yet. Go home first and let's just see what happens.'

Back at Wildgrass we loaded the bikes onto the roof of the bus for the last time. We asked for our bill rather nervously. We said we were going to stay at Wildgrass to the Indians back in Guwahati and they had sucked in their cheeks.

'I am thinking it is too costly for you. For us Indians it is expensive but they put the price up three times for foreigners.'

The bill came. It was the equivalent to thirty-two pounds each and that included everything.

We arrived back in Guwahati and booked into a hotel for the last night. Lee, Glenna and I were travelling to Delhi by the Rajdhani Express train that left at six the following morning. Tim was flying to Calcutta the day after.

Together we went through the motions of a normal night: walking the bazaars, eating dinner, getting ready for bed. We washed each other's hair under the shower, our tears mingling with the water pouring down our faces. We got into bed wanting to snuggle close to each other. The night was too hot and stifling for two bodies to be close. Instead we lay as close as possible with only our fingers touching. I tossed and turned all night willing the morning to come to get this goodbye over and done with.

We were at Guwahati train station at the crack of dawn. The smell was still as intense as one month before, the flies and mosquitoes still in abundance. We picked our way over the sleeping platform to the mailroom and packed up our bikes. As the train pulled in the platform exploded. We boarded and went to find our carriage, seats were important – we had twenty-eight hours in which to sit in them. It was a bum scrum, the porters, the passengers and the sellers shoulder bashing to get through the aisles. We found our seats and went outside to say our last goodbyes to Tim.

Men saying goodbye to men are generally much better than women saying goodbye to women. They know when to become masters of brevity, they keep it simple, tend not to go off on tangents, straight and to the point and economical with their emotions. Tim and Lee were text book. Despite their differences which were very apparent during the seven weeks away together they had fulfilled their dreams and come out of it with a few more skeins of coloured thread to add to life's rich tapestry. They clapped each other on the back, gave each other a strong hug and with one word, 'Laters!' they waved each other goodbye.

Tim and I were left alone, clinging together furiously. There was no point in saying anything. I couldn't even if I wanted to.

Our Hollywood goodbye was suddenly interrupted by a screaming Glenna, her bag with her passport, ticket and money was no where to be found. The whistle for the train's departure blew. Tim ran back to the mailroom to see if she had left it there. By the time he came back the train was pulling out of the station. I hung out of the window trying to grab his hand for one last time. We never made it. His body got swallowed up by the rabble.

'Goodbye Tim and thank you.'

We spent the twenty-eight hours on the Rajdhani Express working out what to do about Glenna's stolen bag. We declared everyone on the train a suspect and set about organising a search ourselves. Not surprisingly the purser was less than helpful. We came across one other westerner sitting a few carriages down from us.

'You gotta sue, no two ways about it. You can't let a reputable service like the Rajdhani get away with it. Nope, you gotta sue, I'm telling ya! Get yourself an attorney, go to the head office in Delhi and demand that they deal with you straight away.'

No prizes for guessing his nationality. Was he travelling in the same country as we were? We were supposed to be on the BA flight out of Delhi that night. I wondered about telling him something I had read only a few days before; the world record for the time spent settling a court action was held by a Pune man who finally won a case which had been filed by his ancestor seven hundred and sixty one years before. But try telling that to a Yank.

I now know that I can cycle anywhere in the world. I survived cycling around Connaught Place in New Delhi. At times it felt like one had more chance of survival cycling criss-cross up the M1 in the opposite direction, but please don't tell my mother that. Connaught Place is a roundabout within a roundabout within a roundabout or as the Indians poetically put it, a son within a mother. I would sooner describe it as a son of bitch within a mother-f…er, but please don't tell my mum that either.

Grand boulevards fed onto this mammoth circular conveyor belt like intravenous drips that stopped for no one. We were often made to swerve out of the way missing a hurtling Ambassador within an inch of our lives. The traffic lights said it all – green light, amber light and then RELAX in red. Never was an order so astute. Above one of the intersections was a sign with a sad face painted on it and the worrying statistics of road accidents that had taken place on that corner:

NUMBER OF ACCIDENTS AT THIS JUNCTION
SINCE BEGINNING OF YEAR: 18

Just as I had finished reading it a loud bang caught my attention. Two mopeds had collided sending both drivers crashing to the ground. Better make that 19. I cycled past the junction as quickly as possible.

We eventually found the British Embassy but only after hiring a motor rickshaw to show us the way. It would have made a good short film titled – A Comedy Of Terrors. Do you know how many motor rickshaws there are in Delhi with the same black painted body and yellow roof? Stopping to wait for a bus to pass, our rickshaw became one of twenty others.

'Where's it gone?'

'There!'

'No, not that one – the one by the newspaper stall.'

'No, ours is much shabbier.'

'QUICK! Get onto the pavement a bus is coming.'

'LEE! Why in God's name did you think it would be easier to cycle?'

'Yeah, we should never have listened to you and just got a bloody cab in the first place.'

Glenna and I had turned into Sybil Fawlty with a bad case of PMT.

'Keep calm ladies. We're nearly there.'

'We're never cycle touring again.'

It was midday. We had eight hours to get Glenna issued with an emergency passport and another ticket. The procedure took seven hours and fifty-five minutes of bureaucratic skullduggery. But who are we to cast the accusing eye? It was our ancestors who gave it to them in the first place.

'What would you like to drink?' Said the smiling B.A. airhostess.

'A double vodka and tonic please.'

The food trolley made its way up the aisle.

'Chicken or vegetarian?'

'Chicken please.'

Half an hour later my stomach started churning in a very musical fashion, followed by fierce spasms. I ran to the loo at the back of the aircraft. Delhi Belly had hit somewhere over Iran. I punched the air.

At last I had been afflicted, I was normal after all.

I made it back to my seat and looked out of the window. At probably the same altitude, a thousand odd miles away, Tim was heading in the opposite direction. I doubted that now we were even in the same continent. For the first time since our goodbye I let myself imagine his face. My mind snapped immediately to his expression when he first told me to come with him to India, blue eyes wide and open.

'Come with me, because if you don't then I know we will never see each other again and I know that I cannot let that happen.'

I wanted to shout at the top of my lungs above the layer of cloud that we were flying across: 'Thank God you said those words. Thank you, thank you, thank you.'

"A memory is what is left when something happens and does not completely unhappen."

Edward de Bono
'The Mechanism of the Mind'

19

HOW LONG IS LONG ENOUGH?

I arrived back in London. I unlocked the door to my house and walked inside. The smell was the same, the usual array of mugs and plates in the sink reassuring me that Ian and Harry's lives were still the same as when I left. I kept myself busy familiarising myself with my home, picking up objects and placing them back a little more to the right or a bit closer to the wall. With this subtle rearranging I was putting my proprietorial stamp back on the place. If I were a dog I would have had a pee against the staircase. I managed to find enough to do to keep me out of the bedroom for a good few hours but unless I slept on the sofa I was going to have to enter sometime. I swallowed the lump in my throat and went inside.

The bed was how Tim had last made it apart from a dent in the duvet where someone had sat to use the phone. All other evidence of him had gone. It was back to being just mine again. I got into bed and toyed with idea of smelling his pillow. I resisted for a good few minutes but gave in, rolling onto his side and burying my head in the pillow. His side? Did I just say – his side? I meant to say the other side of my bed. There was nothing. That's good, I told myself, it's good that there is nothing in this room that belongs to him whatsoever. I liked it like that, no tangible ghosts to leap out at me if I didn't want them to, not even a stray sock that had made its way into my sock drawer. I could even pretend that he was never there.

So this was my plan…it was inevitable that I would feel his absence in the first few weeks, what evolved later would be the telling part. If the pining subsided or if I didn't immediately tear open his letters then I knew to become suspicious of my feelings. If I didn't look forward to his phonecalls or pretended that I wasn't in then I knew to become doubtful of my love for him. Moreover, if his letters became sporadic and his words of missing me more diluted, then I would know to become suspicious of his feelings. Likewise, if he didn't call or if he didn't urge me to come to New Zealand then I would know he was doubtful of his love for me. Great! This was perfect. This was going to be the absolutely foolproof way of knowing what we felt for each other.

I snuggled down in the bed, lying bang, smack in the middle. After half an hour I got up and turned off all electrical appliances at the sockets. Now I come to think about it, I can't remember the humming bothering me when I was with Tim. I could hear the bed squeaking next door. Oh no! My flatmate was having sex. Why didn't I do it more in India? I might never have a chance to do it with Tim again. My chest began to hurt. I rubbed it with the heel of my hand. Polly, don't think about it tonight. I wondered what he was doing now? I couldn't, my powers of imagination only reached as far as Hong Kong. I began to plan my weekend. I got as far as Saturday afternoon then gave up. My ears were still humming. I got out of bed again and leaned out of the window. The humming got louder. A siren passed and an alarm was going off a couple of streets away. Hello London, I'm back. How much did I love this city? How much did I hate it?

I got back into bed this time on my side. It felt better. Now I was really going to concentrate on going to sleep. Sleep was never this elusive when Tim was lying next to me. Instead of counting sheep I was going to sequentially go through every place we slept at during our trip. OK, well first there was the Kathmandu Guest House…

Brr brr, brr brr.

'Hello!'

'Polly?'

'Tim?'

'Polly, when are you coming? Nothing feels right. I feel I am about to scale a mountain but I'm dressed in scuba diving gear.'

'Oh my darling. God I miss you too. I'm lying in our bed and it feels lonely and strange. Why didn't you leave me anything of yours?'

'I didn't think you would want me to. You have my heart.'

'Do I?'

'You know you do. Look in the third drawer down in your pile of T-shirts.'

'I can't come yet Tim, it's too soon.'

'Too soon for what? Polly, you just don't get it do you? In this crazy world I can't believe we have found each other. I'm not going to let you go. If you don't come here then I am coming back to get you.'

I put the phone down and went to the chest of drawers. Third drawer down, sitting on top of my pile of T-shirts was his blue long-sleeved top. I smelled it, it smelt of him. I took it back to our bed and laid it over his pillow then drew it towards me. How much time apart is long enough?

Five months, two weeks, three days and a few hours is how long. I stood at Heathrow Airport with my Mum and Dad, my sister Sophie and Daisy my niece. I don't know if I have ever seen so many tears. Admittedly a fair portion was emitted from Daisy who at four months was not enamoured with the pleasures of Heathrow. God I hate goodbyes. In the last few days I felt thirty going on eleven again. I had kept close to Mum - not quite clutching her skirt. I chose my Last Supper – steak, peas and a baked potato. Even the cabbage reappeared, lodging itself in my throat making it impossible to swallow.

I kissed them all goodbye - then stood away, unable to turn my back. My mum came up for a final touch and we hugged for dear life. I felt horrible and guilty for putting them through the pain of missing me, and for taking away the ray of light, as my mum said, from her life. I steeled my heart and walked away from them. I gave the man my passport and turned to wave for the last time; there they stood, the anchor and mountain of love of my family.

It was July 4th, significant for my departure for two reasons. The first that my new life was beginning on Independence Day, the second that Nostradamus had foreseen the end of the world. I had spoken to Tim earlier in the day.

'I'll see you tomorrow unless the world does really end today.'

'I only have three more hours of today left, I can assure you that nothing momentous feels like it is going to happen. Besides Nostradamus didn't take into account the Polly and Tim story, how could the world end the day before we are re-united?'

The engines started. We were off.

"I have the feeling now that one changes from day to day, and that after a few years have passed one has completely altered. Examine myself as I may, I can no longer find the slightest trace of the anxious, agitated individual of those years, so discontented with herself, so out of patience with others."

George Sands

I think I might have forgotten to mention that my bike is safely stowed away in the hold of this aeroplane. I wonder if the roads have black topping in New Zealand.

LIST OF KIT

1 pair cycling shorts
1 pair cycling leggings
1 pair thermal cycling leggings
1 pair short liners
1 thermal vest
2 T-shirts
2 long-sleeve T-shirts
(1 I left behind in hotel at Lumbini)
1 fleece
1 pair of trousers
1 dress
3 pairs of knickers

1 bra
1 bikini (used as underwear)
1 waterproof windcheater
1 woolly hat
2 pairs of gloves
(1 cycling (lost) and 1 woolly)
1 sun hat
1 helmet
1 sarong
1 pair of sandals
1 pair of Shimano cycling shoes

TOILETRIES

Toothbrush
Toothpaste
Floss
Tube of aqueous cream
Tube of eye cream

Small bottle of shampoo
Tube of moisturiser
2 tubes of sunblock
Super absorbent sports towel
(size of handkerchief)

MEDICAL SUPPLIES

Anti-malarial pills
1 course of general antibiotics
Pack of sterile needles
Diarrohea pills (some chance)
Plasters
Mosquito repellent lotion
Mosquito coils
Arnica cream (for bruises)
Rhus Tox cream
(for tendons, ligaments)
Calendular cream (for saddle sores)

Lipsalve
Water purification tablets
Antiseptic wipes
Sterile dressing
Bandages
Dioralyte
Needle and cotton
Sesame oil for excema on hands
(bought in Kathmandu)

INCIDENTALS

Canon Ixus camera
4 40 exposures IPS film
2 notebooks
2 packets of biros
4 packets of stickers
2 packets of balloons
Knife and fork
Leatherman knife (Tim)
Sleeping bag
(Vango Ultralite 900ML 2
season)
Travel pillow
Thermarest (didn't use)
1 Maglite torch with head strap
(left behind at Eco Camp)
Dictaphone and tapes

Passport
Travellers cheques - £500
(used £360 including presents)
Sunglasses
Glasses
Hindi phrase book
Dice (and later backgammon)
1 packet of Handy Andies
Hairclip
Lipstick (used twice)
Headscarf
2 books: *A Fortune Teller Told Me*,
Tercino Tezziano., *A Thousand
Acres*, Jane Smiley, *Lonely Planet.
India.*

BIKE

Dawes Horizon Tour
Pedals – Shimano PD – T100L
Tyres – Marathon XR – 700 x 32c
Saddle – Acor Conform ladies
(had scooped out groove along the
middle of the saddle, took a bit of
getting used to then became very
comfortable – well, kind of
comfortable).
3 water bottles

Pair of Altura waterproof panniers
1 Karrimor handlebar bag
1 Agu Sport tool bag that fitted
under saddle
2 spare inner tubes
1 Tiptop puncture repair kit
1 set tyre levers
1 front 1 rear Dynamo light
1 bike bag for air travel
1 bell
1 chain and padlock

Other Titles from TravellersEye

Desert Governess

Author: Phyllis Ellis

Editor: Gordon Medcalf

ISBN: 1903070015

R.R.P: £7.99

In 1997 badly in need of a new start in life, Phyllis answered an advertisement: *English Governess wanted for Prince and Princesses of Saudi Arabian Royal Family.* She soon found herself whisked off to the desert to look after the children of HRH Prince Muqrin bin Abdul Aziz al Saud, the King's brother. In this frank personal memoir Phyllis describes her sometimes risky reactions to her secluded, alien lifestyle in a heavily guarded marble palace, allowed out only when chaperoned, veiled and clad from head to foot in black.

Both as a Governess and as a modern western woman she constantly ran up against frustrating prohibitions and unexpected moral codes, only a few of which she could work her way around – usually in the interests of her young royal charges.

Discovery Road

Authors: Tim Garratt & Andy Brown

Editor: Dan Hiscocks

ISBN: 0953057534

R.R.P: £7.99

Their mission and dream was to cycle around the southern hemisphere of the planet, with just two conditions. Firstly the journey must be completed within 12 months, and secondly, the cycling duo would have no support team or backup vehicle, just their determination, friendship and pedal power.

"Readers will surely find themselves reassessing their lives and be inspired to reach out and follow their own dreams."

Sir Ranulph Fiennes, Explorer

Fever Trees of Borneo

Author: Mark Eveleigh
Editor: Gordon Medcalf

ISBN: 095357569
R.R.P: £7.99

This is the story of how two Englishmen crossed the remotest heights of central Borneo, using trails no western eye had seen before, in search of the legendary 'Wild Men of Borneo'. On the way they encounter shipwreck, malaria, amoebic dysentery, near starvation, leeches, exhaustion, enforced alcohol abuse and barbecued mouse-deer foetus.

"Mark has the kind of itchy feet which will take more than a bucket of Johnson's baby talc to cure… he has not only stared death in the face, he has poked him in the ribs and insulted his mother."

Observer

Frigid Women

Authors: Sue & Victoria Riches
Editor: Gordon Medcalf

ISBN: 0953057526
R.R.P: £7.99

In 1997 a group of twenty women set out to become the world's first all female expedition to the North Pole. Mother and daughter, Sue and Victoria Riches were amongst them. Follow the expedition's adventures in this true life epic of their struggle to reach one of Earth's most inhospitable places, suffering both physical and mental hardships in order to reach their goal, to make their dream come true.

"This story is a fantastic celebration of adventure, friendship, courage and love. Enjoy it all you would be adventurers and dream on."

Dawn French

Riding with Ghosts

Author: Gwen Maka

Editor: Gordon Medcalf

ISBN: 1903070007

R.R.P: £7.99

This is the frank, often outrageous account of a forty-something Englishwoman's epic 4,000 mile cycle ride from Seattle to Mexico, via the snow covered Rocky Mountains. She travels the length and breadth of the American West, mostly alone and camping in the wild. She runs appalling risks and copes in a gutsy, hilarious way with exhaustion, climatic extremes, dangerous animals, eccentrics, lechers and a permanently saddle-sore bum.

We share too her deep involvement with the West's pioneering past, and with the strong, often tragic traces history has left lingering on the land.

Slow Winter

Author: Alex Hickman

ISBN: 0953057585

R.R.P: £7.99

Haunted by his late father's thirst for adventure Alex persuaded his local paper that it needed a Balkan correspondent. Talking his way into besieged Sarajevo, he watched as the city's fragile cease fire fell apart. A series of chance encounters took him to Albania and a bizarre appointment to the government. Thrown into an alliance with the country's colourful dissident leader, he found himself occupying a ringside seat as corruption and scandal spilled the country into chaos.

This is a moving story of one man's search for his father's legacy among the mountains and ruin of Europe's oldest, and most mysterious corner.

The Jungle Beat – fighting terrorists in Malaya

Author: Roy Follows
Editor: Dan Hiscocks

ISBN: 0953057577
R.R.P: £7.99

This book describes, in his own words, the experiences of a British officer in the Malayan Police during the extended Emergency of the 1950's. It is the story of a ruthless battle for survival against an environment and an enemy which were equally deadly. It ranks with the toughest and grimmest of the latter-day SAS adventures.

" It tells the story with no holds barred: war as war is. A compelling reminder of deep jungle operations."

General Sir Peter de la Billière

Touching Tibet

Author: Niema Ash
Editor: Dan Hiscocks

ISBN: 0953057550
R.R.P: £7.99

After the Chinese invasion of 1950, Tibet remained closed to travellers until 1984. When the borders were briefly re-opened, Niema Ash was one of the few people fortunate enough to visit the country before the Chinese re-imposed their restrictions in 1987. *Touching Tibet* is a vivid, compassionate, poignant but often amusing account of a little known ancient civilisation and a unique and threatened culture.

"Excellent - Niema Ash really understands the situation facing Tibet and conveys it with remarkable perception."

Tenzin Choegyal (brother of The Dalai Lama)

Heaven & Hell

An eclectic collection of anecdotal travel stories – the best from thousands of competition entries.

"…an inspirational experience. I couldn't wait to leave the country and encounter the next inevitable disaster."   *The Independent*

Travellers' Tales from
Heaven & Hell

Author: Various
Editor: Dan Hiscocks

ISBN: 0953057518
R.R.P: £6.99

More Travellers' Tales from
Heaven & Hell

Author: Various
Editor: Dan Hiscocks

ISBN: 1903070023
R.R.P: £6.99

A Trail of Visions

Guide books tell you where to go, what to do and how to do it. A Trail of Visions shows and tells you how it feels.

"A Trail of Visions tells with clarity what it is like to follow a trail, both the places you see and the people you meet."

Independent on Sunday

"The illustrated guide."
The Times

Route 1: India, Sri Lanka, Thailand, Sumatra

Photographer / Author: Vicki Couchman
ISBN: 1871349338

Editor: Dan Hiscocks
R.R.P: £14.99

Route 2: Peru, Bolivia, Ecuador, Columbia

Photographer / Author: Vicki Couchman
ISBN: 093505750X

Editor: Dan Hiscocks
R.R.P: £16.99

TravellersEye Club Membership

Each month we receive hundreds of enquiries from people who've read our books or entered our competitions. All of these people have one thing in common: an aching to achieve something extraordinary, outside the bounds of our everyday lives. Not everyone can undertake the more extreme challenges, but we all value learning about other people's experiences.

Membership is free because we want to unite people of similar interests. Via our website, members will be able to liase with each other about everything from the kit they've taken, to the places they've been to and the things they've done. Our authors will also be available to answer any of your questions if you're planning a trip or if you simply have a question about their books.

As well as regularly up-dating members with news about our forthcoming titles, we will also offer you the following benefits:

Free entry to author talks / signings
Direct author correspondence
Discounts off new and past titles
Free entry to TravellersEye events
Discounts on a variety of travel products and services

To register your membership, simply write or email us telling us your name and address (postal and email). See address at the front of this book.